Object-Role Modeling Workbook

Data Modeling Exercises using ORM and NORMA

Object-Role Modeling Workbook

Data Modeling Exercises using ORM and NORMA

Terry Halpin

INTI International University

Technics Publications
New Jersey

Published by:

2 Lindsley Road
Basking Ridge, NJ 07920 USA

http://www.TechnicsPub.com

Cover design by Mark Brye

All rights reserved. No part of this book may be reproduced or transmitted in any form or by any means, electronic or mechanical, including photocopying, recording or by any information storage and retrieval system, without written permission from the publisher, except for the inclusion of brief quotations in a review.

The author and publisher have taken care in the preparation of this book, but make no expressed or implied warranty of any kind and assume no responsibility for errors or omissions. No liability is assumed for incidental or consequential damages in connection with or arising out of the use of the information or programs contained herein.

All trademarks are property of their respective owners and should be treated as such.

Copyright © 2016 by Terry Halpin

ISBN, print ed.   9781634621045

ISBN, Kindle ed.   9781634621052

ISBN, ePub ed.   9781634621069

First Printing 2016

Library of Congress Control Number: 2015957065

Contents

Foreword

Dr. Herman Balsters
Associate Professor at the Faculty of Economics and Business
University of Groningen, The Netherlands,
and Director of *Contracts11*

It gives me great personal pleasure to write this foreword, one of the main reasons being that I think that any book written by Terry Halpin is not only a gem to read, but is also an important and practically useful book. I have known Terry personally since I stumbled into an ORM Workshop that was given in Cyprus in 2005. I had never heard about ORM before and I wanted to find out a bit more.

After having attended the first hour at that workshop, I became an immediate addict: my interest in ORM and fact-based modelling has never ceased. This not only has to do with Terry Halpin himself, who I consider as a genius (be it a very humble one) and a great teacher, but also with the artifacts that he has introduced to the data modelling community: the ORM language and the NORMA tool. Before that day in 2005, I had tried very many data modelling languages, and not one of them really satisfied me at all. After being introduced to ORM, I knew right away that this was the way to do it.

ORM is not only very expressive, it is also completely accurate; no ambiguities allowed. ORM's graphical language and the wonderful NORMA tool provide great productivity in analyzing and constructing the most complex data models you could possibly conceive.

I have used ORM both in academia and in business. I have taught hundreds of students how to model and build databases using Terry's books and the NORMA tool. Together with Terry, I have co-authored a number of scientific papers on ORM, and together we chaired and co-chaired the annual ORM Workshop in the years 2010-2013. As a professional consultant and designer of information systems, I have found no other language that is better equipped to do the job than ORM.

In practice, we come across very many badly designed databases. Inspection of those databases often quickly reveals that there was no proper data model at all supporting the database design. These badly designed databases (containing redundancies, lack of semantics, and full of ambiguities) are, unfortunately, more the norm than the exception.

Badly designed databases lead to unadaptable, unintegrated, unmanageable and therefore expensive database implementations. Since databases are at the cornerstone of almost all software systems, it can be regarded as a shame that we do not devote more attention to the role of data modeling when it comes to designing databases.

Luckily we have Terry Halpin and his ORM language to help us shed light on how to arrive at proper, well-understood, and manageable database designs and implementations. An important practical aspect of this book is that it systematically describes how to use the NORMA tool to generate relational database schemas from ORM models, including a treatment of optimization issues.

This particular book is a real complement to other books on ORM written by Terry Halpin. One of the main assets of this book is the wonderful collection of data modeling exercises that Terry has compiled. The exercises are challenging, interesting, and typically based on real-life examples. Another main asset is the detailed explanation of how to use the NORMA tool. I'm sure that even advanced users of ORM and NORMA can benefit greatly from the challenges presented by the modelling exercises and the modelling skills explained in the book using NORMA.

In a way, this book is technical. It's about modelling, and about the difficult aspects of data modelling that you can encounter when trying to model your business domain. Data modelling is never easy, and it involves being both careful and creative. This book shows various pitfalls that you can come across in modelling, and how to solve them. The carefully selected modelling exercises pose a challenge even to the most experienced modeller.

The practical side of this book is that it shows how to systematically use the NORMA tool together with your knowledge of ORM to address these challenges. Once you have experienced these challenges, this book helps you to become a better modeller than you were previously. The carefully crafted solutions to the modeling exercises are described in great detail. As ever, Terry Halpin explains the material—which is often intrinsically complex—as only the great teachers can: he uses simple and straightforward language, and his solutions follow a completely logical sequence of reasoning. I often envy Halpin's style of writing and explaining.

Another asset of the book is the introduction of a completely textual modelling language, which verbalizes the content of ORM diagrams. The verbalizations offered in the book are given in such a way that non-technical domain experts can easily read and write fact-based specifications of the domain to be modelled. Another benefit of these verbalizations is that they offer the possibility to validate the correctness of the models, since such textual specifications can be easily understood, and therefore assessed, by non-technical domain experts. One can easily move back and forth between the verbalizations and their graphical ORM model counterparts.

It seemed difficult for me to consider a book on ORM that could be a real complement to all of the other books on ORM that Terry Halpin has written. This book, however, has convinced me that such a book could be written. Indeed, this is a workbook on ORM: by working through this book you can become a better, accomplished data modeller and database designer than you were previously.

I therefore highly recommend this book to any student, teacher, or professional interested in constructing information systems. The world needs high-quality information systems, and this book provides an excellent resource to help one attain that goal.

Preface

This book focuses on Object-Role Modeling (ORM), a fact-based modeling approach that expresses the information requirements of any business domain simply in terms of objects that play roles in relationships. All facts of interest are treated as instances of attribute-free structures known as fact types, where the relationship may be unary (e.g. Person smokes), binary (e.g. Person was born on Date), ternary (e.g. Customer bought Product on Date), or longer (e.g. Book in Year in Region sold NrCopies).

Fact types facilitate natural expression, are easy to populate with examples for validation purposes, and have greater semantic stability than attribute-based structures such as those used in Entity Relationship Modeling (ER) or the Unified Modeling Language (UML).

All relevant facts, constraints and derivation rules are expressed in controlled natural language sentences that are intelligible to users in the business domain being modeled. This allows ORM data models to be validated by business domain experts who are unfamiliar with ORM's graphical notation. For the data modeler, ORM's graphical notation covers a much wider range of constraints than can be expressed in industrial ER or UML class diagrams, and thus allows rich visualization of the underlying semantics.

This book is a sequel to my previous book *Object-Role Modeling Fundamentals*, and assumes some basic knowledge of the ORM approach as well as some familiarity with the freeware NORMA tool for designing ORM schemas and generating relational database schemas. The relevant background on ORM can be found in my previous book, or in Halpin & Morgan (2008). The relevant back ground on NORMA can be found in my previous book, or from NORMA labs that are freely available from websites such as www.orm.net or www.ORMFoundation.org.

Written in easy-to-understand language, the book illustrates each topic with simple examples, and explains how to use the NORMA tool to implement the ideas discussed. Unlike my previous book, this book includes a large number of practical exercises to promote expertise in the techniques covered, with answers provided to all the exercise questions. It also digs deeper into various ORM topics discussed in my previous book as well as exploring further ORM topics not covered there. Hence, it is intended as a workbook for honing one's skills in ORM.

Chapter 1 provides a brief review of the ORM's conceptual schema design procedure (CSDP), and includes a worked example to illustrate the CSDP as well as NORMA's support for automated verbalization and relational mapping. The chapter concludes with some review exercises to consolidate the ideas discussed.

Chapter 2 discusses in detail how to use the NORMA tool to generate reports that include complete verbalizations of ORM models. It also illustrates the use of vocabulary glossaries that provide complementary documentation to clarify the meaning of terms used in the models.

Chapter 3 provides an overview of ORM's relational mapping procedure, and then discusses how to use the NORMA tool to gain fine control over the ways that names are generated for relational tables and columns, as well as to choose various ways to map subtyping. It then discusses how to annotate relational schema diagrams to capture advanced constraints or derivation rules that are not depicted in NORMA's current relational view notation.

Chapter 4 provides several modeling exercises to consolidate the conceptual modeling and relational mapping techniques discussed in previous chapters. To facilitate hands-on work at various stages of the longer exercises, solutions to previous parts of various exercises are also accessible as downloadable NORMA files.

Chapter 5 discusses the main ways in which an ORM schema may be transformed into an alternative, equivalent ORM schema, and then outlines a conceptual schema optimization procedure that may be used to improve the efficiency of the relational schema generated from ORM. The process of database reengineering is then overviewed. The chapter concludes with a database reengineering exercise that covers the four stages of reengineering an existing, populated database: reverse engineering, schema transformation, relational mapping, and data migration.

Chapter 6 discusses some data modeling patterns for dealing with temporal aspects of information systems (e.g. maintaining history of fact type populations and recording history of role subtype migration), as well as different kinds of collection structures (sets, ordered sets, bags, multisets, and sequences).

Appendix A provides a summary of the ORM graphical notation discussed in the book. This appendix also appeared in my previous book, but is included again for completeness.

Appendix B provides some recommendations for further resources that may be of interest, including some books, journal papers, software, and websites. Publication details of all references cited in the body of the book are included here.

The Answers section just prior to the index provides complete solutions to all the exercise questions in the book.

Although US spelling is used throughout the book, I've adopted Australian punctuation style for quoted expressions and a few other cases. For example, commas or periods appear after, rather than just before, closing quotes, and a comma appears before rather than after contractions such as "e.g." or "i.e.". Moreover, no period is appended to abbreviations whose end letters agree with the full word (e.g. "Mr" and "Dr" are used instead of "Mr." and "Dr.").

Acknowledgements

My sincere thanks go to Dr Herman Balsters, who was kind enough to write the foreword. Many of the exercise questions in this book are based on, or adapted from, a selection of exercise questions I created for use in teaching at INTI International University, and I gratefully acknowledge the permission granted by that university to include such material in this book.

I appreciate the substantial programming work by Matt Curland as lead software developer for the NORMA tool, and acknowledge the pioneering work on fact-based modeling by Sjir Nijssen and Eckhard Falkenberg, who introduced me many years ago to the NIAM variant of the approach. Finally, I thank Steve Hoberman for inviting me to write some ORM books primarily aimed at database practitioners, and for overseeing the publication process.

1 Review of ORM Basics

1.1   Introduction

Object-Role Modeling (ORM) is a fact-based approach to data modeling that expresses the information requirements of any *business domain* or *universe of discourse* (*UoD*) simply in terms of objects that play roles in relationships. All facts of interest are treated as instances of attribute-free structures known as fact types, where the relationship may be unary (e.g. Person smokes), binary (e.g. Person was born on Date), ternary (e.g. Customer bought Product on Date), or longer. Fact types facilitate natural expression, are easy to populate with examples for validation purposes, and have greater semantic stability than attribute-based structures such as those used in Entity Relationship Modeling (ER) or the Unified Modeling Language (UML).

All relevant facts, constraints and derivation rules are expressed in controlled natural language sentences that are intelligible to users in the business domain being modeled. This allows ORM data models to be validated by business domain experts who are unfamiliar with ORM's graphical notation. For the data modeler, ORM's graphical notation covers a much wider range of constraints than can be expressed in industrial ER or UML class diagrams, and thus allows rich visualization of the underlying semantics.

Various software tools are available that enable ORM models to be entered and then used to automatically generate fully normalized relational database models. In this book, the public domain version of the Natural ORM Architect (NORMA) tool is used for this purpose. The NORMA tool is a free plug-in to Microsoft Visual Studio, and may be downloaded from Source Forge at the following website: http://sourceforge.net/projects/orm/. It works with any version of Visual Studio from 2005 onwards, including the Community Edition of Visual Studio 2013 or 2015 (http://www.visualstudio.com/products/visual-studio-community-vs), which is freely available to most users.

This book is a sequel to *Object-Role Modeling Fundamentals* (Halpin, 2015), and assumes some familiarity with both ORM and the NORMA tool. The relevant background on ORM is available in that book and can also be found in the second edition of *Information Modeling and Relational Databases* (Halpin & Morgan, 2008). For the relevant background on NORMA, preferably see *Object-Role Modeling Fundamentals*, Alternatively, you can download the NORMA lab files that are accessible at either www.ORMFoundation.org or www.orm.net.

This chapter provides a quick review of the basic procedures for designing ORM models, and illustrates them with a worked example. Later chapters discuss further aspects of ORM and NORMA that were not covered in my previous book, and provide modeling exercises for which answers are provided in the back of the book. Appendix A provides a glossary of the ORM graphic notation, and Appendix B lists further resources.

1.2   ORM's Conceptual Schema Design Procedure

Table 1.1 lists the main steps in ORM's *Conceptual Schema Design Procedure* (*CSDP*). For large information systems, the business domain is first divided into prioritized sub-domains, the CSDP is applied to each, and then the resulting subschemas are merged to produce the global conceptual schema. In practice, all seven steps are usually performed for each component of the model as it is discussed with the domain expert, before moving on to the next component of the model.

To seed the data model, we begin with *data use cases* that provide concrete examples of the kinds of facts that are of interest. These data use cases may take the form of sample output reports, input forms, or queries that the information system is required to manage. In Step 1 of the CSDP, the domain expert verbalizes the sample facts in any natural way, and then we formally re-verbalize the information as *atomic facts*, which cannot be decomposed into smaller facts. An atomic fact is either elementary or existential. An *elementary fact* applies a logical *predicate* to a sequence of one or more objects (e.g. The Moon named 'Phobos' orbits the Planet named 'Mars'). An *existential fact* simply asserts an object's existence (e.g. There exists a Planet named 'Mars').

Table 1.1   ORM's Conceptual Schema Design Procedure (CSDP)

Step Nr	Description
1	1a: Verbalize familiar examples in natural language (domain expert's task)
	1b: Re-verbalize the examples as atomic facts (modeler's task)
2	Draw the fact types
	and apply a population check
3	Check for entity types that should be combined
	and note any arithmetic derivations
4	Add uniqueness constraints
	and check the arity of the fact types
5	Add mandatory role constraints
	and check for logical derivations
6	Add value constraints, set-comparison constraints (i.e. subset, exclusion, and equality constraints), and subtyping
7	Add frequency, ring, value-comparison, cardinality and deontic constraints, then add any textual constraints and perform final checks

An object is either an entity (e.g. an individual person or country), a domain value (e.g. a family name or a country code) or a data value (e.g. a character string or number). Each entity is identified by a reference scheme that relates it directly or indirectly to one or more domain values. An entity type may have more than one reference scheme (e.g. a country may be identified by a code or a name), but exactly one of these is chosen as the preferred reference scheme. The simplest kind of reference scheme identifies an entity by its relationship to a single domain value—in this case the preferred reference scheme of an entity type may be abbreviated by appending its reference mode in parentheses. For example, Country(.Code) abbreviates the reference fact type Country has CountryCode.

1.3   A Worked Example

To illustrate the CSDP, we now consider designing a simplified information system to manage details about employees. Table 1.2 and Figure 1.1 shows extracts from two reports about employees, one in tabular form and the other in graphical form. For simplicity, person names are treated here as single character strings. We will use these reports as data use cases to help design the information system.

Table 1.2   Extract from a report about employees

EmployeeNr	Name	Title	Gender
101	Ann Jones	Dr	F
102	Sue Wong	Mrs	F
103	John Smith	Dr	M
104	Beth Morgan	Ms	F
105	Tom Jones	Mr	M
106	Ann Bloggs	Ms	F
107	John Smith	Mr	M

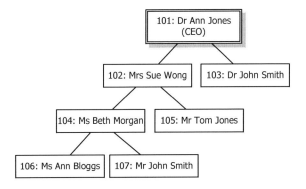

Figure 1.1   Extract from an employee organization chart

As a third data use case for this business domain, suppose that the following example query is of interest. Here, a subordinate of an employee either reports to that employee (and hence is a direct report of that employee) or reports to some other subordinate of that employee. For the sample data, this query returns the result shown:

List the employee number and name of the subordinates of employee 102.

⇨   104   Beth Morgan
105   Tom Jones
106   Ann Bloggs
107   John Smith

Our task is to design a data model to support these information requirements. We begin by verbalizing (typically with the help of a domain expert) the sample information as fact instances expressed in atomic sentences, and documenting the meaning of any terms used in the domain that might possibly be misunderstood by users. For example, using "Nr" as shorthand for "Number", the first row of data in Table 1.2 may be verbalized as shown below. Since more than one employee may have the same person name (e.g. 'John Smith') we identify employees by their employee numbers.

The Employee with EmployeeNr 101 has the PersonName 'Ann Jones'.
The Employee with EmployeeNr 101 has the PersonTitle 'Dr'.
The Employee with EmployeeNr 101 has the Gender with GenderCode 'F'.

By removing the specific object terms in these fact instance verbalizations, we generalize these instances to the following underlying fact types (kinds of fact). Here, the names of object types (kinds of objects) start with a capital letter, and the preferred reference schemes for the entity types are appended as shorthand reference modes in parentheses. Domain values such as person names and person titles are essentially self-identifying, so their reference schemes are empty. The other facts in rows 2 through 7 of the Table 1.2 are instances of one of these three fact types.

Employee(.Nr) has PersonName().
Employee(.Nr) has PersonTitle().
Employee(.Nr) has Gender(.Code).

Similarly, the new information in the organization chart in Figure 1.1 may be verbalized as follows. We do not bother to restate the person name facts, since these were included in the verbalization of the tabular report. For clarity, we expand "CEO" to "chief executive officer".

The Employee with EmployeeNr 101 is chief executive officer.
The Employee with EmployeeNr 102 reports to the Employee with EmployeeNr 101.
The Employee with EmployeeNr 103 reports to the Employee with EmployeeNr 101.
etc.

Each fact conveyed by the organization chart is an instance of one of the following fact types. There is only one instance of the first fact type because at most one employee is the CEO. Each of the six links in the organization chart depicts an instance of the second fact type.

Employee(.Nr) is chief executive officer.
Employee(.Nr) reports to Employee(.Nr)

The fact types may be displayed and populated as shown in Figure 1.2. Entity types are displayed as named, solid, rounded rectangles, with their reference modes underneath in parentheses. Value types are displayed as named, dashed, rounded rectangles. A fact role is a part played by an object in a fact. A role is displayed as a box connected by a line to the object type that hosts it.

An ordered set of all the roles in a fact type is a logical predicate. Predicate readings are displayed alongside, and are read from left to right or top to bottom, unless the reading direction is reversed by an arrow-head. Here four binary fact types (each with two roles), and one unary fact type (with one role) are displayed, along with their sample populations shown in accompanying fact tables. In this example, all object types are simply identified, so each role corresponds to a column in the associated fact table.

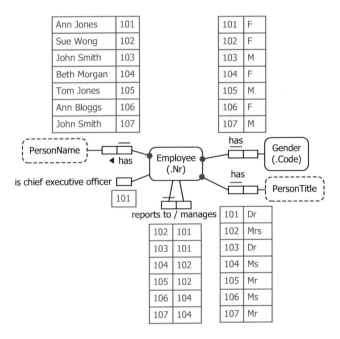

Figure 1.2   **Displaying and populating the fact types, and adding some constraints**

If desired, the same fact may be expressed in more than one way by using different predicate readings. For example, the fact that Employee 102 reports to Employee 101 may also be expressed by saying that Employee 101 manages Employee 102. In Figure 1.2 this is indicated by including both the forward predicate reading "reports to" and the inverse predicate reading "manages" separated by a slash "/".

The next phase of the design procedure involves declaring constraints that apply to the data model. If for each state of the fact base, each entry in a role's fact column may appear in that column only once, then the role has a simple uniqueness constraint. For a binary or longer fact type, this is depicted as a bar beside the role box.

Since ORM fact types are always populated by sets of facts (not multisets), the role in a unary fact type implicitly has a uniqueness constraint, so there is no need to display a uniqueness constraint bar for it. The lack of a uniqueness constraint on a role indicates that duplicates may appear in its fact column. See Figure 1.2 for several examples.

If for each state of the fact base, each instance in the population of an object type must play a given role, then the role is said to be mandatory for that object type. A mandatory role constraint is displayed by placing a large dot at one end of the line connecting the role to its object type shape. The dot may be displayed at the object type end (as shown in Figure 1.2) or at the role end.

Constraints are validated with the domain expert by verbalizing them in a controlled natural language, and by checking whether they conform to sample data populations. For example, the uniqueness and mandatory role constraints depicted in Figure 1.2 may be automatically verbalized as follows.

Each Employee has **exactly one** PersonName.
It is possible that more than one Employee has **the same** PersonName.
Each Employee has **exactly one** Gender.
It is possible that more than one Employee has **the same** Gender.
Each Employee has **exactly one** PersonTitle.
It is possible that more than one Employee has **the same** PersonTitle.
Each Employee reports to **at most one** Employee.
It is possible that some Employee manages **more than one** Employee.

The phrase "exactly one" combines both uniqueness (at most one) and mandatory (at least one). The lack of a uniqueness constraint on a role is verbalized by indicating that the same object may appear more than once in any given population of that role.

Constraints may also be verbalized in a negative way to indicate what counts as a violation of the constraint, and a counterexample to the constraint may be used to illustrate such a violation. Asking the domain expert whether such counterexamples are allowed is a good way of checking constraints that are doubtful.

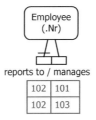

Figure 1.3   Checking a uniqueness constraint with a counterexample

For example, the uniqueness constraint on the reporting fact type may be verbalized in negative form as "**It is impossible that some** Employee reports to **more than one** Employee", and checked using the counterexample shown in Figure 1.3 which provides a concrete case of an employee reporting to more than one employee.

The conceptual schema design procedure includes a set of instructions for detecting other constraints that may apply. For example: Are there any other relationships of interest, especially functional (many-to-one, or one-to-one) relationships? In this case, the data suggests that some person titles are restricted to a single gender (e.g. 'Mr' is restricted to males, while 'Mrs' and 'Ms' are restricted to females). When this restriction is confirmed by the domain expert, we add the functional fact type PersonTitle is restricted to Gender, as shown in Figure 1.4.

The sample data also suggests that there are only two possible gender codes ('M' for male, and 'F' for female) and four possible person titles {'Dr', 'Mr', 'Mrs', 'Ms'}. Assuming that the domain expert agrees to the gender code list but adds 'Lady, 'Prof' and 'Sir' as possible person titles, we add the value constraints displayed as {'M', 'F'} as {'Dr', 'Lady, Mr', 'Mrs', 'Ms, 'Prof', 'Sir'} in Figure 1.4.

As a design option, suppose that the client wants the implemented database to include a table that lists all the possible person titles. To meet this requirement, we declare PersonTitle to be an independent object type, as shown by the appended exclamation mark "!" in Figure 1.4.

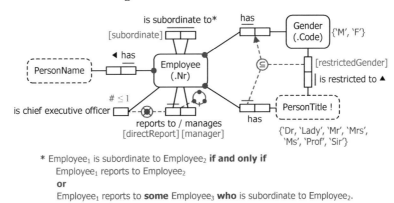

Figure 1.4   Refining the conceptual schema

Other steps in the design procedure prompt us to add the further constraints shown in Figure 1.4. The join subset constraint depicted as a circled subset operator symbol connected to relevant roles verbalizes as shown below. For example, this constraint prevents one from assigning the title 'Mrs' to an employee of male gender.

> **If some** Employee has **some** PersonTitle **that** is restricted to **some** Gender
> **then that** Employee is of **that** Gender.

The "# ≤ 1" role cardinality constraint on the unary fact type ensures that at any point in time there is at most one chief executive officer. The circled and crossed mandatory dot connected to the CEO and reporting roles depicts an exclusive-or constraint over these roles, indicating that each recorded employee must play exactly one of these roles. These constraints may be verbalized as follows:

> **For each population of** "Employee is chief executive officer",
>   **the number of** Employee **instances is at most** 1.

> **For each** Employee, **exactly one of the following holds:**
>   **that** Employee is chief executive officer
>   **that** Employee reports to **some** Employee.

The circle with three dots and a stroke attached to the reporting fact type depicts an acyclic ring constraint indicates that the reporting relationship is acyclic. This may be verbalized as follows:

> **No** Employee **may cycle back to itself via one or more traversals through**
> Employee reports to Employee.

The derived fact type Employee is subordinate to Employee is introduced to support the query example discussed earlier. The asterisk appended to its predicate reading indicates that instances of the fact type are derived from other facts rather than simply being asserted. The following derivation rule used to infer instances of this fact type is shown below the diagram, and prepended by an asterisk.

> * Employee$_1$ is subordinate to Employee$_2$ **if and only if**
> Employee$_1$ reports to Employee$_2$
> **or**
> Employee$_1$ reports to **some** Employee$_3$ **who** is subordinate to Employee$_2$.

This derivation rule is recursive, since the "is subordinate to" predicate is used in both the head and the body of the rule. The acyclicity constraint on the reporting fact type also involves recursion, and may be enforced by checking that the transitive closure of the reporting fact type is irreflexive. Given the derivation rule for the fact type Employee is subordinate to Employee it follows that the transitive closure of the Employee reports to Employee fact type is the extension of the derived fact type Employee is subordinate to Employee.

The acyclicity constraint on the Employee reports to Employee fact type may be checked most efficiently by materializing (storing the population of) the derived Employee is subordinate to Employee fact type, and implementing the constraint incrementally. In other words, when the reporting fact type is updated, only the updates to the population of the derived fact type need be checked for irreflexivity, rather than recomputing the full transitive closure and testing that for irreflexivity.

Hence, for efficiency reasons, the ring fact type Employee is subordinate to Employee is declared to be derived and stored (shown graphically by appending a double asterisk to its predicate reading) and irreflexive (shown graphically by attaching a constraint circle with a dot and stroke). See Figure 1.5. The irreflexive ring constraint verbalizes as follows:

No Employee is subordinate to **the same** Employee.

If desired, a fact role may be given a role name, for use in rules that reference the role, or to control the names of columns generated when mapping the ORM schema to a relational database schema. Diagrammatically, role names appear in square brackets next to the role that they name. Figure 1.4 includes three examples of role names: directReport, manager, and subordinate.

By default, alethic constraints on derived fact types are implied, and are displayed in the usual color (violet). In Figure 1.5, the irreflexive ring constraint shape is colored red, indicating that the constraint on the derived fact type is asserted. The acyclic ring constraint on the asserted fact type Employee reports to Employee is now implied, so may be omitted as shown in Figure 1.5, as no code is needed to enforce implied constraints.

Figure 1.5   **The asserted, irreflexive constraint implies that reporting is acyclic**

Purely for informational purposes, you may wish to display implied constraints on an asserted fact type. In this case, the implied constraints should be colored green. The reports to predicate in Figure 1.5 is both functional (uniqueness constraint on its first role) and acyclic (by implication), which implies it is strongly intransitive (Exercise 1.3 invites you to prove this). The strong intransitivity constraint may be verbalized thus: **If** Employee$_1$ reports to **some** Employee$_2$ **then it is not true that** Employee$_1$ **is indirectly related to** Employee$_2$ **by repeatedly applying this fact type.**

Figure 1.4 omitted the implied strong intransitivity constraint. Figure 1.6 uses a combined icon in green color to display both implied ring constraints (acyclic and strongly intransitive) on the reporting fact type.

is subordinate to**
[subordinate]

Employee
(.Nr)

reports to / manages
[directReport] [manager]

Figure 1.6   The acyclic and strongly intransitive ring constraints are implied

The conceptual schema for the example business domain is now complete, and may be mapped to various targets systems (e.g. a relational database or a deductive database) for implementation.

Figure 1.7 shows a NORMA screenshot of the ORM schema with implied constraints omitted, as well as the relational schema diagram generated by NORMA after assigning appropriate data types to the ORM value types. In the relational schema diagram, mandatory (non-nullable) columns are displayed in bold type and optional (nullable) columns are shown in non-bold type. Primary keys are marked "PK", and foreign keys "FKn". The primary key of the PersonTitle table displays as "value", which is a reserved word in several SQL dialects, so NORMA adds double quotes to it to make it a delimited identifier when mapping to SQL code.

The ORM exclusive-or constraint, value constraint, frequency constraint, join subset constraint and irreflexive constraint are not displayed on the relational schema diagram but can be specified in SQL after generating the SQL code for the schema.

For a discussion on using NORMA to generate SQL code from relational schemas, see either Appendix A of my previous book (Halpin, 2015) or NORMA Lab1 which is downloadable from either www.ORMFoundation.org or www.orm.net. Using the mapping procedure discussed there, and choosing SQL server as the mapping target, the current version of the public domain version of the NORMA tool generates the Data Definition Language (DDL) code shown after Figure 1.7.

By default, NORMA maps characters to the national character set (for SQL server this means Unicode), so the string data types begin with 'n' for national (e.g. nchar rather than char), and string values are prepended by 'N' (e.g. N'Dr' instead of 'Dr'). For this example, I chose to map the ORM schema to SQL Server 2008, which uses the bit datatype to store Boolean values. Currently, NORMA maps SubordinateOfEmployee as a base table. You can manually edit this to create a view instead.

As you can see, NORMA generates SQL code for basic ORM constraints such as uniqueness, mandatory role and value constraints, but does not yet generate SQL code for several other ORM constraints.

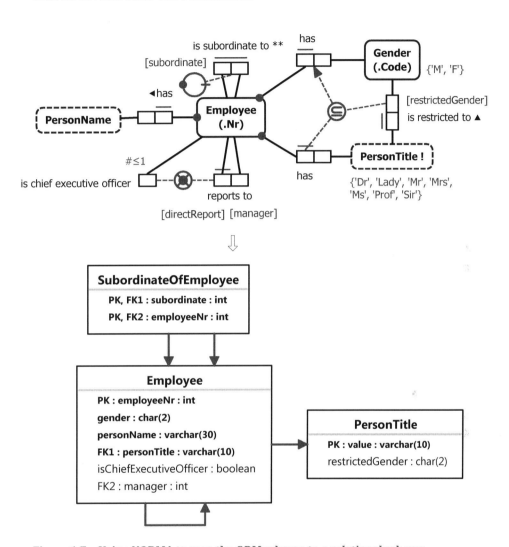

Figure 1.7   Using NORMA to map the ORM schema to a relational schema

```
CREATE SCHEMA ORMModel1
GO
GO


CREATE TABLE ORMModel1.Employee
(
employeeNr int NOT NULL,
gender nchar(2) NOT NULL,
```

```
personName nvarchar(30) NOT NULL,
personTitle nvarchar(10) CHECK (personTitle IN (N'Dr', N'Lady', N'Mr',
N'Mrs', N'Ms', N'Prof', N'Sir')) NOT NULL,
isChiefExecutiveOfficer bit,
manager int,
CONSTRAINT Employee_PK PRIMARY KEY(employeeNr),
CONSTRAINT Employee_gender_RoleValueConstraint1 CHECK (gender IN (N'M',
N'F'))
)
GO


CREATE TABLE ORMModel1.PersonTitle
(
"value" nvarchar(10) CHECK ("value" IN (N'Dr', N'Lady', N'Mr', N'Mrs',
N'Ms', N'Prof', N'Sir')) NOT NULL,
restrictedGender nchar(2),
CONSTRAINT PersonTitle_PK PRIMARY KEY("value"),
CONSTRAINT PersonTitle_restrictedGender_RoleValueConstraint1 CHECK
(restrictedGender IN (N'M', N'F'))
)
GO


CREATE TABLE ORMModel1.SubordinateOfEmployee
(
subordinate int NOT NULL,
employeeNr int NOT NULL,
CONSTRAINT SubordinateOfEmployee_PK PRIMARY KEY(subordinate, employeeNr)
)
GO


ALTER TABLE ORMModel1.Employee ADD CONSTRAINT Employee_FK1 FOREIGN KEY
(personTitle) REFERENCES ORMModel1.PersonTitle ("value") ON DELETE NO
ACTION ON UPDATE NO ACTION
GO


ALTER TABLE ORMModel1.Employee ADD CONSTRAINT Employee_FK2 FOREIGN KEY
(manager) REFERENCES ORMModel1.Employee (employeeNr) ON DELETE NO ACTION ON
UPDATE NO ACTION
GO


ALTER TABLE ORMModel1.SubordinateOfEmployee ADD CONSTRAINT
SubordinateOfEmployee_FK1 FOREIGN KEY (subordinate) REFERENCES
ORMModel1.Employee (employeeNr) ON DELETE NO ACTION ON UPDATE NO ACTION
GO


ALTER TABLE ORMModel1.SubordinateOfEmployee ADD CONSTRAINT
SubordinateOfEmployee_FK2 FOREIGN KEY (employeeNr) REFERENCES
ORMModel1.Employee (employeeNr) ON DELETE NO ACTION ON UPDATE NO ACTION
GO
```

In this example, the uniqueness constraints are implemented as primary key constraints, and simple mandatory role constraints are implemented not null constraints and foreign key references. Value constraints are implemented as check clauses.

With the current version of NORMA, the other ORM constraints need to be coded manually. For example, if the target SQL system supports assertions, the join subset constraint may be coded as follows:

```
create assertion personTitle_gender_constraint
    check ( not exists
        ( select *
        from Employee join PersonTitle
            on Employee.personTitle = PersonTitle."value"
        where gender <> restrictedGender )
```

If the target system does not support assertions, the join subset constraint can be coded using triggers. SubordinateOfEmployee may be coded as a materialized view using SQL's union operator within a recursive query definition. For a detailed discussion of SQL and examples of coding various ORM constraints in SQL, see chapters 12 and 13 of Halpin & Morgan (2018).

As discussed in the next chapter, the conceptual and physical schemas are usually supplemented by supporting documentation to clarify the meaning of any aspects of the schema terminology that might possibly be misunderstood.

Since the conceptual model (both schema and sample population) may be verbalized unambiguously in a controlled natural language that is readily intelligible to domain experts, the conceptual model can be validated with domain experts without their needing to view and understand the schema diagrams. For data modelers, however, the expressive graphical notation is very useful for capturing and visualizing the business data requirements in a compact form and for seeing how different aspects are connected.

☐   *Exercise 1.3*

_____

1. Prove the implication that a fact type that is both functional and acyclic is also strongly intransitive.

   Hint: Assume that the implication does not apply, and then show that this leads to a contradiction.

   (Answers to exercise questions are included in the Answers section at the back of the book.)

2. Write SQL code to enforce the exclusive-or constraint that verbalizes as follows:

   For each Employee, **exactly one of the following holds:**
       that Employee is chief executive officer
       that Employee reports to **some** Employee.

Hint: If using the bit datatype for Boolean values, **true** is rendered as **1** and false as **0**. For example, to test that an employee is CEO you use the condition is-ChiefExecutiveOfficer = 1. Boolean data types were introduce in ISO standard SQL in SQL:1999. If your SQL supports the ISO standard syntax for Boolean values, the same condition may be coded as isChiefExecutiveOfficer **is true**.

1.4   Review Exercises

This section includes several short exercises to consolidate basic understanding of ORM modeling as discussed in this review chapter. You can complete the exercises either by hand or by using an ORM tool such as NORMA or the ORM2 stencil for Microsoft Visio. Answers are included in the Answers section at the back of the book.

Exercise 1.4

1. An ORM conceptual schema diagram with sample population is shown below. For simplicity, reference schemes are omitted, object types are named "*A*".."*C*", and predicates are named "**R**".."**V**". Fact tables appear next to their fact types. Constraints are identified as *C1..C10*.

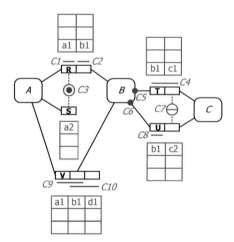

Each of the following requests applies to the same database population shown (i.e. treat each request as if it was the first to be made on this population). For convenience, extra blank rows are included for manual updates of the table data (erase such updates before attempting the next part of the exercise).

Fact types are shown in prefix notation (i.e. predicate first). For each request, indicate the response of the Conceptual Information Processor (CIP). If the request is legal, write "accepted". Otherwise, indicate a constraint violated (e.g. "C2 violated"). If more than one constraint is violated by a request, indicate only one of the constraints violated.

(a) add: **R** a2 b1
(b) add: **T** b1 c1
(c) add: **T** b1 c2
(d) add: **V** a2 b1 d1
(e) add: **R** a2 b2
(f) *delete:* **R** a1 b1
(g) begin

    add: **T** b2 c1

    add: **U** b2 c2

    end

2. Which of the following is FALSE (circle the relevant letter)?
    A.   Entities may typically change their state.
    B.   An atomic fact is either elementary or existential.
    C.   Each binary fact type requires at least one uniqueness constraint.
    D.   No fact type can have overlapping uniqueness constraints.
    E.   An inclusive-or constraint can apply to more than two roles.

3. An ORM conceptual schema diagram with sample population is shown below. For simplicity, reference schemes are omitted, object types are named "A".."D", and predicates are named "R".."V". Fact tables appear next to their fact types. Constraints are identified as *C1..C9*.

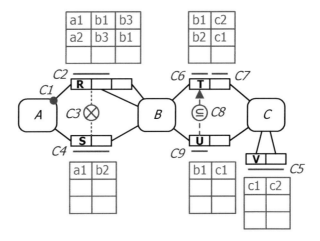

Each of the following requests applies to the same database population shown (i.e. treat each request as if it was the first to be made on this population). For convenience, extra blank rows are included for manual updates of the table data (erase such updates before attempting the next part of the exercise).

Fact types are shown in prefix notation (i.e. predicate first). For each request, indicate the response of the Conceptual Information processor (CIP). If the request is legal, write "accepted". Otherwise, indicate a constraint violated (e.g. "C2 violated"). If more than one constraint is violated by a request, indicate only one of the constraints violated.

(a) add: **T** b3 c2
(b) add: **R** a1 b1 b2
(c) add: **S** a3 b3
(d) add: **T** b3 c3
(e) add: **S** a1 b1
(f) begin
    add: **S** a1 b3
    add: **S** a1 b4
    end
(g) add: **U** b3 c1
(h) *delete:* **T** b1 c2
(i) add: **V** c2 c1

4. The following schema is population inconsistent (it cannot be populated without generating a contradiction). Constraints are numbered C1..C7. Indicate in the space provided which constraint contradicts (is population inconsistent with) the constraint specified.

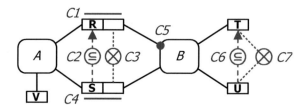

(a) Which constraint contradicts (i.e. is population inconsistent with) constraint C6?

(b) Which constraint contradicts (i.e. is population inconsistent with) constraint C3?

5. The following table shows an extract of population data for some countries (based on 2015, with figures rounded to the nearest thousand). For detailed reports on past, present and projected future population data, see the United Nations Population Division website http://esa.un.org/unpd/wpp/.

Country	Male Population	Female Population	Total Population	Majority Gender
Australia	11 976 000	11 993 000	23 969 000	Male
China	708 977 000	667 072 000	1 376 049 000	Male
French Guiana	164 000	164 000	268 000	
India	679 548 000	631 503 000	1 311 051 000	Male
Latvia	904 000	1 067 000	1 971 000	Female
Qatar	1 624 000	612 000	2 236 000	Male
United States of America	159 494 000	162 280 000	321 774 000	Female
...	...	...	...	...

(a) Specify an ORM schema for this report using binary fact types only. Allow that other countries may be included.

(b) Remodel your schema using a ternary fact type for the male and female population data.

(c) The following table shows an extract of projected, future, total population data for various countries and years (no data is recorded for projected male and female populations). Specify an ORM schema for this report using a ternary fact type. Allow that other years may be added as well.

Country	Projected Population 2030	Projected Population 2050	Projected Population 2100
Australia	28 482 000	33 496 000	42 389 000
China	1 415 545 000	1 348 056 000	1 004 392 000
French Guiana	381 000	546 000	891 000
India	1 527 658 000	1 705 333 000	1 659 786 000
Latvia	1 806 000	1 593 000	1 278 000
Qatar	2 781 000	3 205 000	3 170 000
United States of America	355 765 000	388 865 000	450 385 000
...	...	...	...

6. The following reports are extracted from an information system used to manage course tutorials for the current quarter only. To save space, only a small amount of data from each report is shown here.

In the following table about buildings and rooms, "capacity" means the number of people the room can seat. Some rooms might not actually be used for tutorials.

Building Nr	Building Name	Nr of Elevators	Room		
			Room Nr	Capacity	Air-conditioned
1	Armstrong	0	B12	40	No
			G20	50	Yes
2	Asimov	2	223	50	Yes
3	Tolkien	2	223	90	Yes
			345	50	Yes

Further details are in the following table. The credit point value for a course is recorded whether or not the course has students enrolled in it. Each student either takes a course or tutors in a course (possibly both).

Full enrollment listings are kept. Some courses don't have tutorials (e.g. CS202).

If a student tutors in a course, the number of tutorial groups he/she tutors is recorded.

Course		Enrollment			Students who tutor in that course		
Code	Credit	Count	Student Nr	Student Name	Student Nr	Student Name	Nr of Groups
CS100	10	90	20001	Potter, Harry	10005	Smith, John	3
			20002	Jones, Eve			
			...	...			
CS101	8	120	20002	Jones, Eve	00007	Bond, James	3
			20005	Seldon, Hari	10005	Smith, John	2
			...	...			
CS202	10	35	10005	Smith, John			
			10017	Smith, John			
			...	...			

The following table lists details about tutorial groups. *Each tutorial group meets only once a week.* At any time, a room has at most one tutorial. In this system, we do *not* record who belongs to each tutorial group, or who tutors each tutorial group.

Each tutorial lasts one hour. Hour slots are identified by codes (e.g. Mon-10am) which you should treat as simple identifiers (do not treat them as composite). Rooms are listed in a single column in this table, but you should model their identification scheme as composite.

Course	Tutorial Group Code	Hour Slot	Room
CS100	A	Mon-2pm	1-B12
	B	Mon-2pm	2-223
	C	Tue-10am	1-B12
CS101	A	Mon-2pm	3-223
	B	Tue-9am	3-345
	...	...	...

(a)   A conceptual schema for the first two reports is set out below, minus constraints and derivation rules. Add all relevant *uniqueness* (internal or external) and *mandatory role* (simple or disjunctive) *constraints*. If a fact type
is derived, add an asterisk to it on the diagram and include a *derivation rule*
for it.

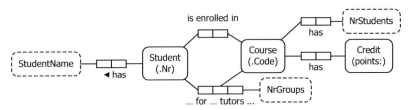

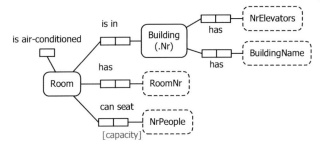

(b)   Add a schema diagram for the third report about tutorial groups. Do not
use subtyping. Include all uniqueness and mandatory role constraints.

2 Documenting Models

2.1 Generating Model Reports

ORM models entered in the NORMA tool are automatically verbalized in controlled natural language, so are essentially self-documenting. For the purposes of model review and validation by domain experts, the NORMA tool includes a report generator to automatically generate reports of the model verbalizations in hypertext markup language (HTML), including check boxes for obtaining written agreement by the domain expert.

This section discusses how to generate such a report, using the Employee model from chapter 1 as an example. If you have not already done so, enter the Employee ORM model in NORMA and save it as Employee.orm. Alternatively, you can use any other ORM model that you have created in NORMA.

First let's create a folder to store your NORMA reports. In Windows Explorer right-click a parent folder of your choice (e.g. Documents), then from the context menu choose New > Folder and rename the folder called "New Folder" as "NORMA Reports", then right-click that folder and similarly create a subfolder called Employee (or whatever name you prefer).

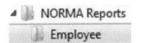

In Visual Studio, open the ORM file for which a report is required by selecting the menu options File > Recent Files and selecting your relevant .orm file (e.g. Employee.orm). If the relevant ORM file is not listed in your recent files, use Windows Explorer to locate the file (e.g. in the Projects folder with the Visual Studio folder) then double-click the file to open it.

With your ORM model displayed in the Documents Window, right-click an empty space and from its context menu select Generate Report > HTML Report (see next page for a screenshot using Employee.orm as the sample file).

The Verbalization Report Generator dialog box appears. Press the "…" button that is displayed at the right of the Output Directory field, browse to your relevant Reports folder, then press OK (see next page).

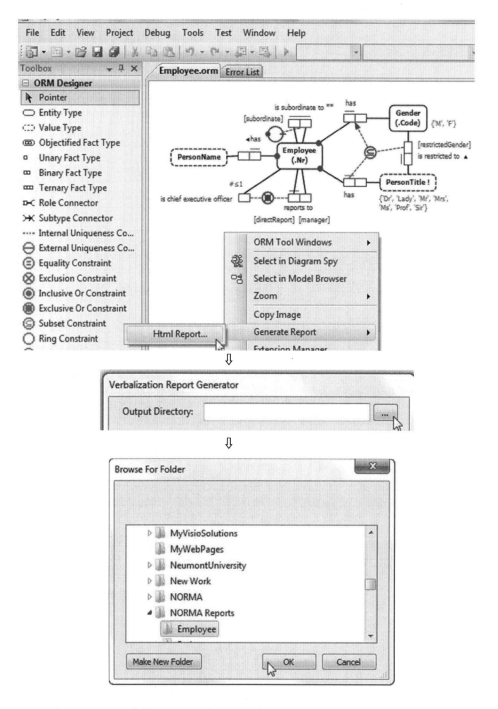

Your relevant report folder is now listed as the Output Directory (see next page). Check boxes allow you to control what is included in the report. By default, all boxes are checked. Accept this default, and press the Generate Report button.

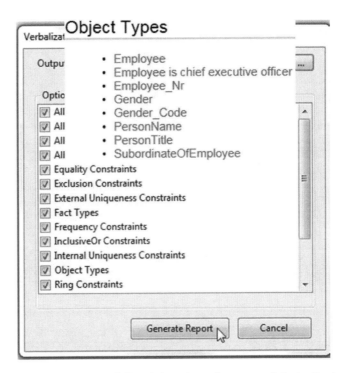

The report is now generated (it might take a few seconds). An Explorer window appears with the generated results placed in your report folder.

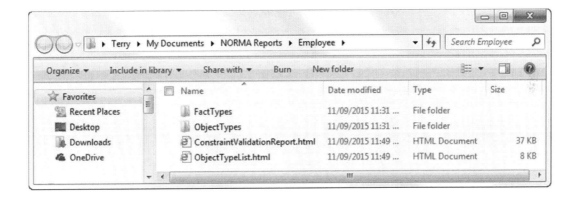

Double-click the file ObjectTypeList.html to open the Object Type List. A list of all the object types in your ORM model is now displayed in alphabetical order in your Web browser. As well as the object types, NORMA currently includes in this list the names of some fact types (see next page).

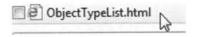

Object Types

- Employee
- Employee is chief executive officer
- Employee_Nr
- Gender
- Gender_Code
- PersonName
- PersonTitle
- SubordinateOfEmployee

The report contains hyperlinks for navigating around the ORM model. When you hover the cursor over a model element, the cursor becomes a hand shape, and you can simply mouse-click to jump to details for that element. For example, if you click Employee a page about Employee appears.

Object Types

- Employee
- Employee

"Employee" Object Type ↑

Summary

Employee **is an entity type**.
  Reference Scheme: Employee has Employee_Nr.
  Reference Mode: .Nr.
  Data Type: Numeric: Signed Integer.

Fact Types

- Employee has Employee_Nr.
- Employee has Gender.
- Employee has PersonName.
- Employee has PersonTitle.
- Employee is chief executive officer.
- Employee reports to Employee.
- Employee is subordinate to Employee.
    Instances of this fact type are stored immediately after they are derived.

Related Types

- Employee is chief executive officer
- Employee_Nr
- Gender
- PersonName
- PersonTitle

Super Types

- There are no items for this section.

Sub Types

- There are no items for this section.

Click any element on that page to jump to details about that element. For example, if you click the fact type Employee reports to Employee a page about that fact type appears.

- Employee reports to Employee.
- Employee is subordinate to Em

⇩

"EmployeeReportsToEmployee" Fact Type ↑

Summary

Employee reports to Employee.

Role Players

- Employee

Constraints

InternalUniquenessConstraint9

Type: InternalUniquenessConstraint
Verbalization:

  Each Employee reports to **at most one** Employee.

ExclusiveOrConstraint1

Type: InclusiveOrConstraint
Verbalization:

  For each Employee, **exactly one of the following holds:**
  that Employee is chief executive officer;
  that Employee reports to **some** Employee.

Click the up-arrow on the header to return to the top level of the report. Now click Constraint Validation to open the Constraint Validation Report. You could also open this report by double-clicking ConstraintValidationReport.html in the report folder.

"EmployeeReportsToEmployee" Fact Type ↑

⇩

ORMModel1.

Object Types

- Employee

Verbalization Report Contents

1. Object Types
2. Constraint Validation

All the fact types in the model are listed in alphabetical order as well as their constraint verbalizations. A check box is placed beside each constraint so the reviewer may indicate whether he or she agrees with the constraint. As with the Object Types report, you can navigate via hyperlinks by clicking any element for details about it. Use the scroll bar at the right to move up or down through the report.

To save space for the below screenshot, I've scrolled to the end of the report and displayed here just the details of the final fact type. I've also checked the two constraint boxes to show I agree with their verbalizations. Notice the Signature line. This is for the reviewer to sign on a printed version of the report, after checking all the boxes for the constraints that he or she agrees with.

"SubordinateOfEmployee" Fact Type ↑

Summary

Employee is subordinate to Employee.
Instances of this fact type are stored immediately after they are derived.
Derivation Note: *Employee1 is subordinate to Employee2 if and only if Employee reports to Employee2 or Employee1 reports to some Employee3 who is subordinate to Employee2.*

Role Players

- Employee

Constraints

☑ InternalUniquenessConstraint11

Type: InternalUniquenessConstraint
Verbalization:

It is possible that some Employee is subordinate to **more than one** Employee **and that for some** Employee$_1$, **more than one** Employee is subordinate to **that** Employee$_1$.
In each population of Employee is subordinate to Employee, **each** Employee, Employee **combination occurs at most once.**
This association with Employee, Employee **provides the preferred identification scheme for** SubordinateOfEmployee.

☑ RingConstraint1
Type: RingConstraint
Verbalization:

No Employee is subordinate to **the same** Employee.

Signature

You can print the html report from your Web browser. If you wish to have a copy of the report in other formats, return to the top level of the report, press Ctrl+AC to copy all its contents to the clipboard, then open your word processor (e.g. Microsoft Word) and paste the report into it. You can now save and print the report from your word processor.

The Reports folder includes two subfolders, one for fact types and one for object types. Double-click a folder to get a list of its element files. Then double-click any file to view its details. For example, double-clicking FactTypes then Employ- eeHasGender.html gives the following:

⇓

"EmployeeHasGender" Fact Type ↑

Summary

Employee has Gender.

Role Players

- Employee
- Gender

Constraints

InternalUniquenessConstraint5

Type: InternalUniquenessConstraint
Verbalization:

Each Employee has **at most one** Gender.

SimpleMandatoryConstraint3

Type: SimpleMandatoryConstraint
Verbalization:

Each Employee has **some** Gender.

SubsetConstraint1

Type: SubsetConstraint
Verbalization:

If some Employee has **some** PersonTitle **that** is restricted to **some** Gender **then that** Employee has **that** Gender.

2.2   Vocabulary Glossaries

To facilitate understanding of models by general users, it helps to supplement the documentation provided by model diagrams and model reports with vocabulary glossaries that explain the meaning of critical terms (e.g. object type names, and role names) and fact type readings whose meaning might not be obvious.

For example, Table 2.1 lists entries starting with the letter "A" from the term dictionary for the Fact Based Modeling (FBM) metamodel that is currently under discussion by the FBM Working Group.

Table 2.1   Extract from FBM Metamodel Term Dictionary

Term	Definition/Description

Alethic constraint	A restriction that cannot be violated by any state or state transition of the conceptual model. It may be expressed positively as a necessity, or negatively by indicating an impossibility.
	
	Examples:
	    Each Person was born on at most one Date.
	    No Person is a parent of itself.

Alethic modality	Modality of necessity and possibility.
Arity	Number of roles in a relationship type (number of arguments of a predicate): 1 = unary, 2 = binary. 3 = ternary, etc.
Asserted fact	Fact instance that is simply asserted (declared to be the case) rather than being derived from other facts. All asserted facts are atomic. Synonyms: primitive fact; base fact; extensional fact.
Asserted fact type	Fact type, each of whose population instances is an asserted fact. Synonyms: primitive fact type; base fact type; extensional fact type.
Asserted subtype	Subtype where membership of population instances in that subtype is simply asserted rather than being derived from properties of its supertype(s).
Atomic fact	An elementary fact or an existential fact. An atomic fact cannot be decomposed into smaller facts involving exactly the same object types. Synonym: irreducible fact.
Atomic fact type	Fact type, each of whose instances is an atomic fact.

One use of role names in an ORM schema is to control names of columns in the relational schema that is automatically generated from the ORM schema. As a supplement to our Employee model, Table 2.2 includes explanations for role names that might be misunderstood.

Table 2.2   Clarifying the meaning of some role names in our Employee model

Role Name	Explanation
directReport	If employee *e1* reports to employee *e2*, then *e1* is a direct report of *e2*, and *e2* is the manager of *e1*.
manager	An employee who manages at least one other employee.
subordinate	If employee *e1* reports either to employee *e2* or to some employee *e3* who ultimately (via a chain of one or more intermediate managers) reports to *e2*, then *e1* is a subordinate of *e2*.

Similar explanations may be provided for object type names and fact type readings whose meaning is not obvious. The NORMA tool allows you to add *informal descriptions* for such terms. You can choose to display these descriptions as tooltips on the ORM diagram and also copy such descriptions into a glossary table in your word processor.

For example, open the Employee model, select the PersonTitle shape, and press the down-arrow at the right of the InformalDescription property in the Properties window. In our example, we limit person titles to those in prefix position, so add the following text as the informal description: "A prefix added to a person's name as a mark of respect or in acknowledgment of their official or professional status" and press Enter.

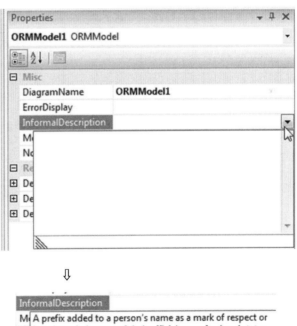

To have this description displayed as a tooltip, choose Tools > Options... from Visual Studio's main menu to open the Options dialog. Scroll down, and select ORM

Designer. In the ORM Designer pane, scroll to Appearance, and double-click the Show Description Tooltips property to toggle it from False to True, then press OK.

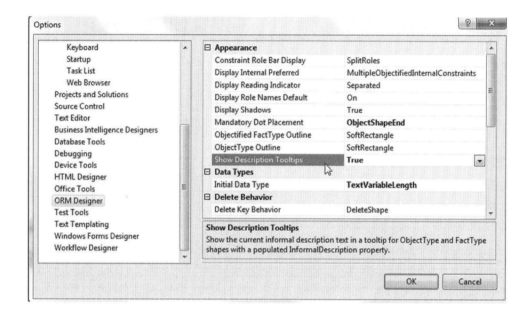

Now hover the mouse over the PersonTitle shape on the ORM diagram. A tooltip now appears, displaying the informal description that you entered for this model element.

Now select the PersonTitle shape and view its verbalization in the ORM Verbalization Browser. The informal description is included in the verbalization.

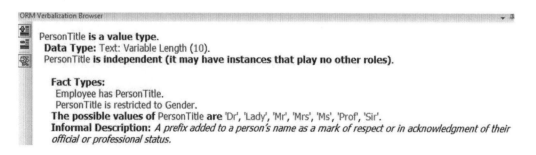

Similarly, you may add informal descriptions to any other object types or fact types. You can also copy the description text from either the verbalizer or the informal description property into a glossary table in your word processor.

3 Relational Mapping

ORM includes a Relational mapping (Rmap) procedure for mapping an ORM schema to a relational database schema. Mainly to assist you with relational mapping aspects of later exercises, this chapter provides an overview of the basic steps in the Rmap procedure. It also discusses some relational mapping options supported by NORMA that were not covered in my previous book.

3.1   Overview of ORM's Relational Mapping Procedure

The main steps in ORM's Rmap procedure are summarized in Table 3.1. NORMA performs most of these steps automatically, generating a relational schema in fifth normal form by default. The most important ideas behind the way Rmap groups ORM fact types into relational table schemes are contained in steps 1 and 2, and in this section we briefly illustrate those steps. Some aspects of the other steps are discussed in later sections of this chapter. For a detailed discussion of the full Rmap procedure, including related procedures such as the Total Table Procedure, see chapter 11 of Halpin & Morgan (2008).

Table 3.1   Main steps in ORM's Rmap procedure

Step	Description
0	Mentally erase all explicit preferred identification schemes, treating compositely identified object types as "black boxes". Indicate any absorption-overrides (separation or partition) for subtypes.
1	Map each fact type with a compound internal uniqueness constraint to a separate table.
2	Group fact types with functional roles attached to the same object type into the same table, keyed on the object type's identifier. Map 1:1 cases to a single table, generally favoring fewer nulls.
3	Map each independent object type with no functional roles to a separate table.
4	Unpack each "black box column" into its component attributes.
5	Map all other constraints and derivation rules. Subtype constraints on functional roles map to qualified optional columns, and those on nonfunctional roles map to qualified subset constraints. For each absorbed, asserted subtype with functional roles or no roles, add a Boolean attribute in its absorption table to indicate membership in the subtype. Nonfunctional roles of independent object types map to column sequences that reference the independent table.

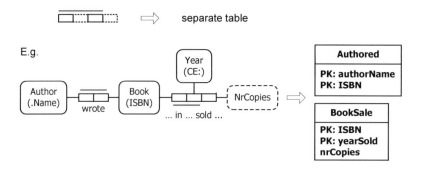

Figure 3.1   Illustration of Rmap Step 1

In Rmap Step 1, we map each fact type with a compound internal uniqueness constraint to a separate table. For example, in Figure 3.1, the fact types Author wrote Book and Book in Year sold NrCopies each have a compound internal uniqueness constraint, so each of these fact types maps to a separate table scheme as shown. NORMA's relational diagram notation displays mandatory (not nullable) columns in bold, and prepends primary keys columns by "PK:".

In Rmap Step 2, we group fact types with functional roles attached to the same object type into the same table, keyed on the object type's identifier. For a 1:1 fact type with one mandatory and one optional role, we group the fact type into the table for the object type hosting the mandatory role, since this mapping choice results in fewer nulls. For example, in Figure 3.2 the head politician fact type is grouped into the Country table rather than the Politician table.

In NORMA's relational notation, columns other than primary key columns whose non-null entries are unique (not duplicated) are prepended by a uniqueness constraint marker "Un" (n ≥ 1). Foreign key references are depicted as an arrow from the source table to the target table. For example, the foreign key reference in Figure 3.2 constrains each politicianName entry in the Politician table to also occur in the headPolitician column of the Country table. If you hover the mouse over the foreign key arrow, NORMA shows a tooltip identifying the precise columns involved.

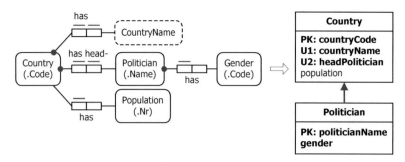

Figure 3.2   Illustration of Rmap Step 2

Exercise 3.1

1. Manually map the following ORM schema to a relational schema. Ignore setting of data types. As described later in the chapter, the NORMA tool can perform this mapping for you automatically. However, try to map it yourself manually before using NORMA for this purpose.

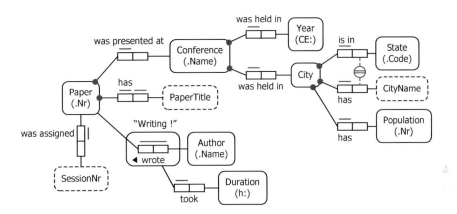

2. Manually map the following ORM schema to a relational schema. Ignore setting of data types. Annotate the diagram with relational equivalents of the ORM sub- set and exclusion constraints and the subtype derivation rule using any notation of your choice. A suggested notation using footnotes for such annotations is dis- cussed in the final section of this chapter.

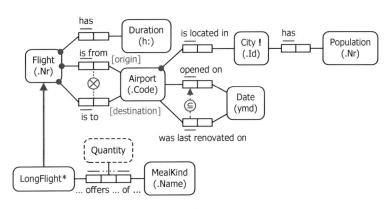

* **Each** LongFlight **is defined as a** Flight **that** has Duration >= 5.

3.2   Downloading and Viewing a Sample NORMA Model

Figure 3.3 shows an ORM schema and a view of the relational schema generated from it by NORMA. The subtypes MaleEmployee and FemaleEmployee are derived (as shown by the asterisks) and Executive is an asserted subtype. Notice that the fact type MaleEmployee is husband of FemaleEmployee is 1:1, with both roles optional. This maps to the Employee table column maleEmployeeFemaleEmployeeNr.

In principle, either role could be used for the mapping, but NORMA chose to map from the perspective of MaleEmployee. To confirm this, select the column and note that MaleEmployee is listed before FemaleEmployee in the verbalization.

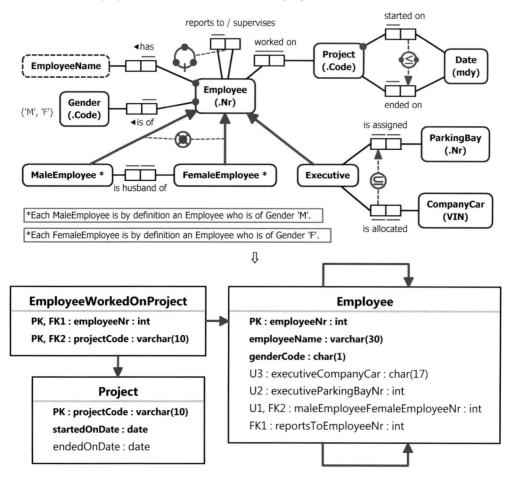

Figure 3.3   An ORM schema and its relational view in the NORMA file Employee.orm

This sample model is accessible as the file Employee.orm, which you can download from the Web using the following link: http://1drv.ms/1Mrf8eT. We will now use this example to illustrate various relational mapping options in the NORMA tool.

To best benefit from this discussion, you should perform the actions discussed your-self using NORMA. To begin, either download and open the Employee.orm file or create it yourself using techniques discussed in my previous book.

When you open the file, the ORM schema is displayed in the document window. Select the Relational View tab at the bottom of this window to display the relational schema diagram (If the Relational View tab is absent, right-click an empty space in the document window, select Extension Manager from the context menu, check Relational View and press OK).

By default, the data types for each table column are displayed in the relational view. In the Properties window for the relational view, double-click the Display-DataTypes property to toggle its setting from True to False.

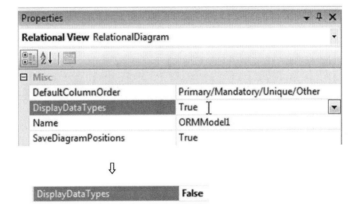

The relational view now displays without the data types, allowing a more com-pact display.

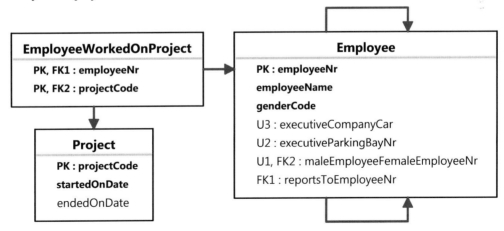

3.3   Controlling Table and Column Names in NORMA

NORMA automatically supplies default names for *m:n* fact types, *n*-ary fact types (*n* > 2), and objectified types. These names become the names of the tables generated from these fact types, assuming the objectified predicate has a spanning uniqueness constraint (i.e. covering all the roles). For the current model, the Employee worked on Project fact type is the only fact type named in this way. You can see that the table scheme generated from this fact type is also named EmployeeWorkedOnProject.

NORMA allows you to edit the relational names directly on the relational view, but we now discuss how to control the names generated for various relational model elements by modifying settings on the ORM schema itself.

Select the Employee tab at the bottom of the Document window to return to the ORM schema, then select the Employee worked on Project fact type, open its Properties Window, edit its Name property to "EmployeeProjectWork", and press Enter.

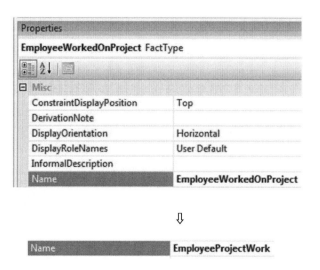

Now click the Relational View tab to see the modified relational schema diagram. The relevant table scheme has been renamed to "EmployeeProjectWork".

Select the EmployeeProject and Project tables, and nudge them closer to the Employee table as shown on the next page.

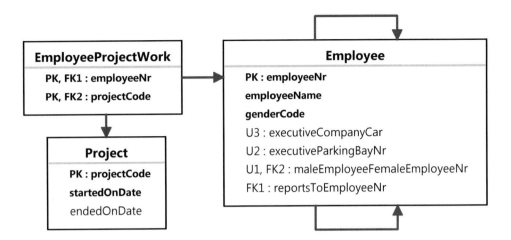

Another way to modify table names is to use the Abbreviation facility discussed later for column names. However, the table names are now satisfactory, so let's move onto the column names. As already indicated, you can edit the column names directly on the relational view, but lets' see how to control the column names by modifying the ORM schema.

Select the Employee tab below the document window to return to the ORM schema. Now select the role hosted by Date in the Project started on Date fact type, and edit its Name property to startDate.

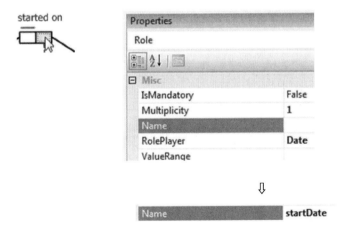

Similarly, edit the role name for the role hosted by Date in the Project ended on Date fact type to endDate.

Similarly, edit the role name for the second role hosted by Employee in the Employee reports to Employee fact type to manager.

Similarly, edit the role name for the role hosted by FemaleEmployee in the fact type MaleEmployee is husband of FemaleEmployee fact type to wife.

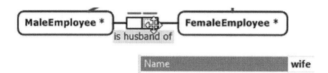

Role names appear on the diagram inside square brackets near their role. Select each such displayed role name and move it closer to the role as shown in the following ORM schema diagram.

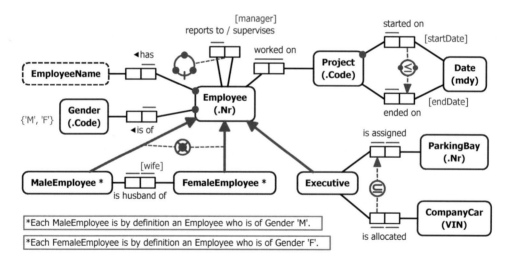

Now click the Relational View tab below the document window to view the relational schema diagram. The columns generated from named roles have been renamed, as shown on the next page.

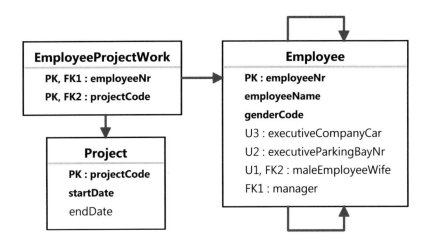

To see the precise columns involved in a foreign key reference, hover the mouse over the arrow depicting the foreign key reference to invoke the tooltip with this information. For example:

Let's now see how to use abbreviations to further control the generation of column names. Click the Employee tab on the document window to return to the ORM schema. In the ORM Model Browser, expand Name Generation Settings, then Name Generation Defaults, and then Relational Names, and select Column Specific. The Properties Window now offers many options for controlling names. In the Abbreviations property, select the "..." button to open the Abbreviations dialog.

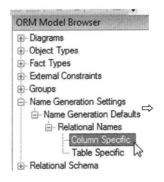
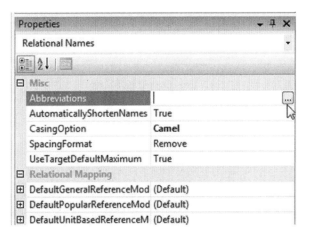

Expand Object Type Abbreviations, select New, then scroll down the drop-down list to Employee, and press Enter. Then enter "Emp" in the Abbreviation field and press the OK button.

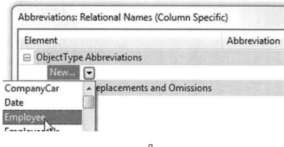

⇩

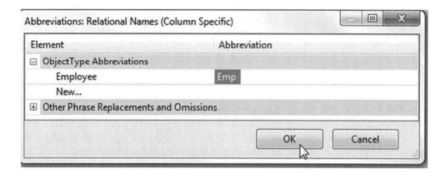

Click the Relational View below the document window to return to the relational schema diagram. The primary identifier column for the object type Employee is now shortened from "employee" to "empNr" in the Employee table and the EmployeeProjectWork table. It is not desired to abbreviate the table name "Employee" in the same way, but if you did want to do this you could choose Table Specific and enter the abbreviation there in a similar way.

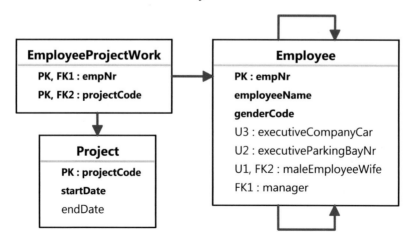

Notice that "employeeName" and "maleEmployeeWife" are not abbreviated. To abbreviate these, return to the Abbreviations dialog, expand the Other Phrase Replacements and Omissions option. This option allows abbreviations for any phrases whatsoever, regardless of whether they are object type identifiers. As this feature is quite powerful, use it with care.

Now select New, then type "Employee" in the text box that appears, then enter "Emp" in the Abbreviation field and press OK. Now all the column-specific entries of "Employee" are abbreviated to "Emp" while leaving name of the Employee table unabbreviated.

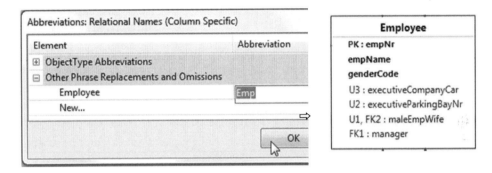

Since this is stronger than the earlier object type abbreviation for Employee, we no longer need that earlier abbreviation. To delete it, expand ObjectTypeAbbreviations, select "Emp" in the Abbreviation column, press the Delete key, and then press OK.

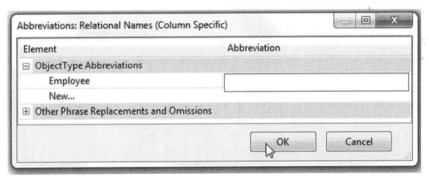

We now consider some further naming format options. In the Properties Window of the ORM schema, expand DefaultPopularReferenceModeNames. This allows you to change the format used by default when an object type with a popular refmode has a role that maps to a primary key or another column.

By default, when mapping to a column, the refmode name is appended to the entity type name (e.g. projectCode and employeeNr). This is reasonable for this model, so leave the defaults unaltered. The defaults for general and unit-based refmodes may also be modified using this window. However, let's leave them unaltered.

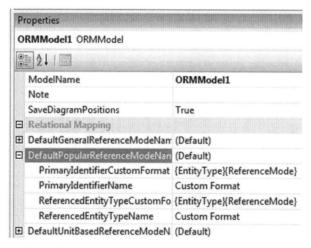

Instead, we will modify a specific case (Gender) to override the default behavior. On the ORM schema, select the Gender entity type. In the Properties Window, select ReferencedEntityTypeCustomFormat. It's set to {EntityType}{ReferenceMode} indicating this format will be used when a role for that object type maps to a column that is not a simple primary key, e.g. genderCode. Select {ReferenceMode} and press Delete to reduce the format to {EntityType}.

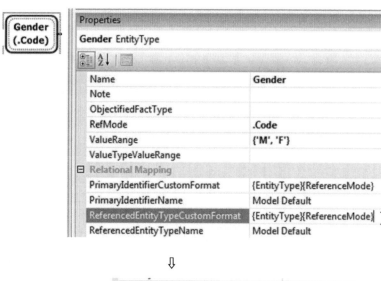

Now "gender" is used instead of "genderCode" for the relational column, as shown on the next page.

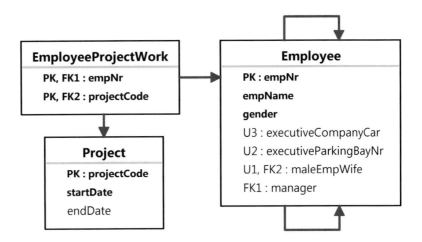

By default, NORMA generates table names in Pascal case, and column names in camel case, with spaces removed (e.g. "projectCode" is camel case). I prefer to leave these defaults unaltered, but let's see how to change them if desired.

In the ORM Model Browser, select Name Generation Settings then Name Generation Defaults then Relational Names then Table Specific. In the Properties Window, click the CasingOption dropdown list to see the choices available.

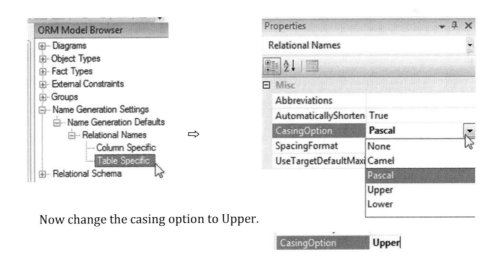

Now change the casing option to Upper.

All tables now have their names displayed with all letters in upper case, as shown on the next page.

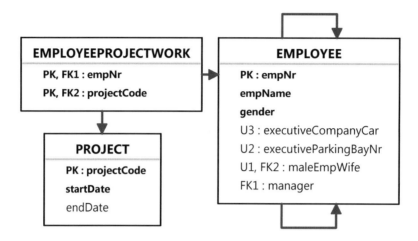

Try the other options to see the effect. Then revert back to Pascal case.

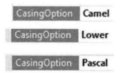

In the ORM Model Browser relational name generation settings, select Column Specific. In the Properties Window, click CasingOption and change its entry from Camel to Pascal.

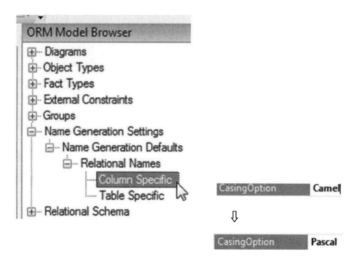

All columns now have their names displayed in Pascal case, as shown on the next page.

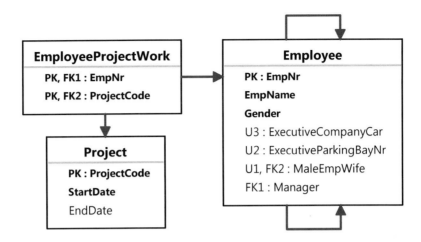

Try the other options to see the effect. Then revert back to camel case.

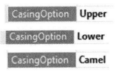

Still on Column Specific settings, select SpacingFormat to see the options. The default Remove option removes spaces between words. Change the SpacingFormat to Retain to retain the spaces between words.

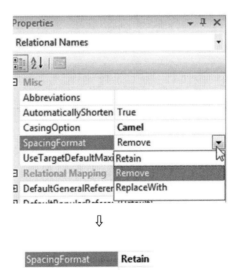

Multi-word columns now have their names displayed with spaces between the words, as shown on the next page.

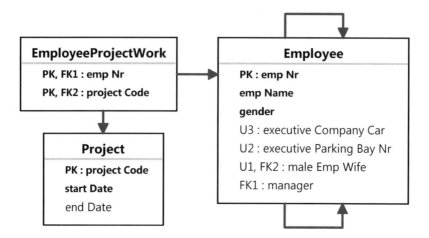

Now change the SpacingFormat to ReplaceWith. A SpacingReplacement option now appears just below. For this property, enter the underscore "_" character to be used as a word separator in column names (choose another character if you like). Notice the effect.

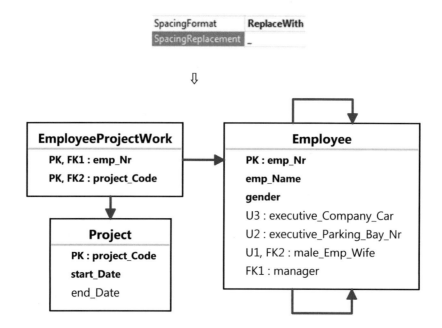

Now reset the column specific spacing format back to Remove to return to our earlier display.

3.4   Subtype Mapping Options

We now consider some *subtype mapping options*. By default, NORMA *absorbs* functional roles (with a simple uniqueness constraint) on subtypes back into their top level supertype for relational mapping. So the executiveCompanyCar, executiveParkingBayNr and maleEmpWife columns are absorbed into the Employee table as shown.

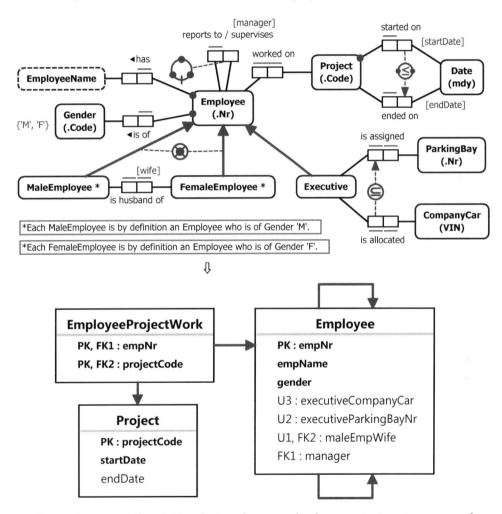

Currently, NORMA's relational view does not display annotations to capture the ORM acyclic, value-comparison, exclusive-or and subset constraints or the derivation rules for the MaleEmployee and FemaleEmployee subtypes. We discuss how to add such annotations manually in the next section of this chapter.

Moreover, NORMA currently fails to include a Boolean isExecutive attribute in the Employee table. Since Executive is an asserted subtype with no mandatory role constraint (simple or disjunctive), such a Boolean attribute is needed to record whether an employee with no company car or parking bay is an executive. This is a known bug with NORMA that should be fixed at a later date. In the meantime, one way to avoid this bug is to map Executive's functional fact types into a separate table for executives. To do this, select the Executive subtype on the ORM schema then in its Property Window change its AbsorptionChoice from Absorbed(All Paths) to Separate.

The relational view now displays with a separate Executive table to identify those employees who are executives and record the functional facts specific to executives. Besides fixing the bug, the separate table for Executive might be preferable (e.g. it reduces the amount of nulls and could be easier for users to understand).

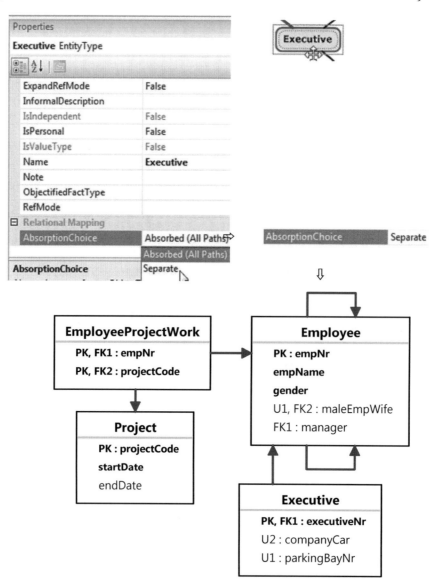

If you wish, you could similarly create a separate table for MaleEmployee to record which employees are males as well as their wife (if any). Similarly, you could also create a separate table for FemaleEmployee simply to record which employees are female. However, let's choose not to do this.

As yet another subtype mapping option, NORMA allows you to partition map a supertype whose subtypes collectively form a partition (i.e. the subtypes are mutually exclusive and collectively exhaustive). In our example, the subtypes of Employee do not form a partition, because the exclusive-or constraint between the MaleEmployee and FemaleEmployee subtyping links does not include the subtyping link to the Executive subtype.

To demonstrate the partition map option with our example, we'll use a modified version of the model with the Executive subtype removed. First, save your Employee.orm model by pressing the Save icon in the main menu.

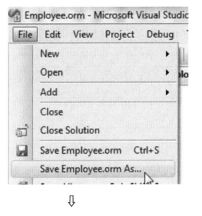

Now click the File option in the main menu, then click the Save Employee.orm As … option from its submenu to open the Save File As dialog. Then edit the filename to Employee2.orm and press the Save button.

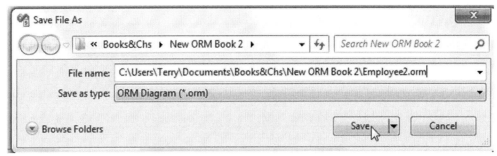

Now drag the mouse over the Executive subtypes and its two attached fact types to select them, then press the Delete key, and then press Yes to each of the element deletion requests that now appear (the next page shows the first two deletions).

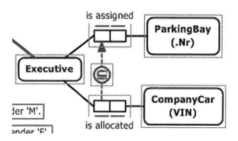

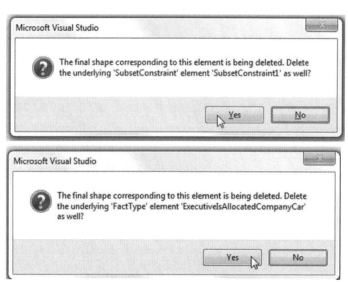

Continue clicking Yes to the subsequent deletion requests to delete the fact type 'ExecutiveIsAssignedCompanyCar', and the object types ParkingBay, CompanyCar and Executive. The Employee2.orm schema now displays as shown below.

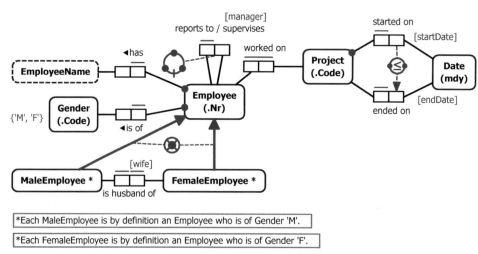

Now select the Employee entity type and look at its Properties sheet. The Relational Mapping section now shows an AbsorptionChoice property. Click the down-arrow to open the drop-down list for this property, and select Partitioned.

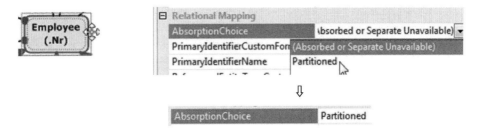

Select the Relational View tab below the Document window to see the new version of the relational view. The former Employee table has been replaced, and its empName, gender and manager attributes have now been moved down into each of the MaleEmployee and FemaleEmployee tables.

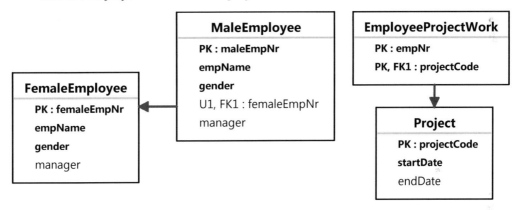

The maleEmpWife attribute of the former Employee table has been moved into the MaleEmployee table, and renamed femaleEmpNr. To rename this attribute directly on the relational view, select the attribute and edit its Name property to wifeEmpNr.

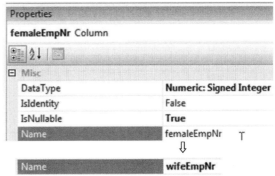

The relational view immediately reflects this change, as shown below. The foreign key reference directed from MaleEmployee.wifeEmpNr to FemaleEmployee.femaleEmpNr ensures that each recorded wife is a female employee.

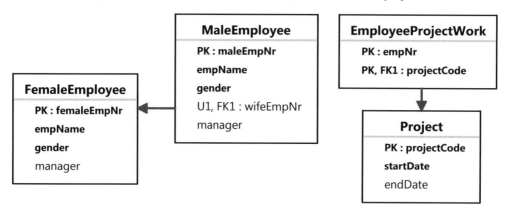

One disadvantage of this partition map is that there is now no constraint to ensure that each empNr in the EmployeeProjectWork table is also included as either a femaleEmpNr in the femaleEmployee table or as a maleEmpNr in the MaleEmployee table. So if you choose the partition map option, you need to cater for that constraint manually. With the former design, this constraint was effectively handled simply by a foreign key reference to the Employee table.

To revert to the former relational design, select Employee in the ORM schema and edit its AbsorptionChoice property to Remove Partition (Try to Absorb Subtypes).

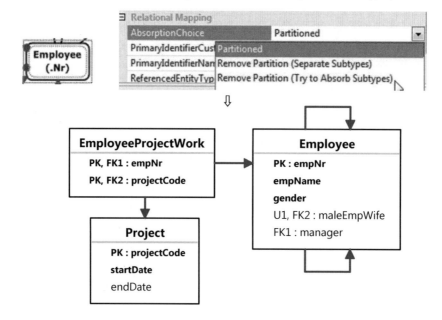

For some application domains, the partition map option is extremely useful (e.g. partitioning a phone directory table for the USA into fifty tables, one for each state). In general however, care should be used when using the partition map option.

3.5   Annotating Relational Schemas

Figure 3.4 redisplays the ORM schema and final relational view of the Employee.orm model discussed in the previous section. Currently, NORMA does not display relational equivalents for the value, acyclic, set-comparison and subset constraints or the subtype definitions.

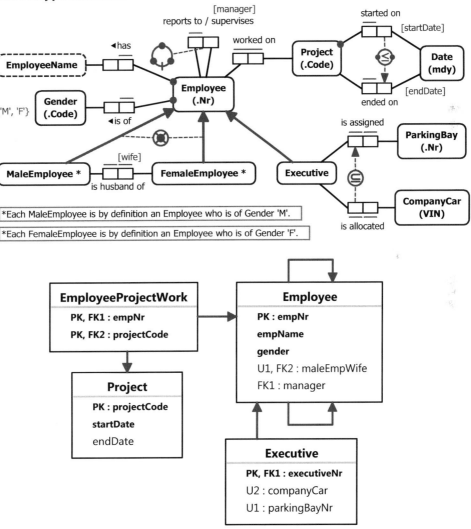

Figure 3.4   The Employee ORM schema and its relational view in NORMA

For documentation purposes, and to facilitate manual editing of the SQL code generated to ensure its completeness, it is desirable to manually annotate the relational view to declare the missing semantics. The easiest way to do this is to copy the relational view from NORMA into a tool such as Microsoft Visio or Microsoft Word and then add the annotations manually. Figure 3.5 shows one way of specifying the required annotations. For this example, I added the annotations in Visio.

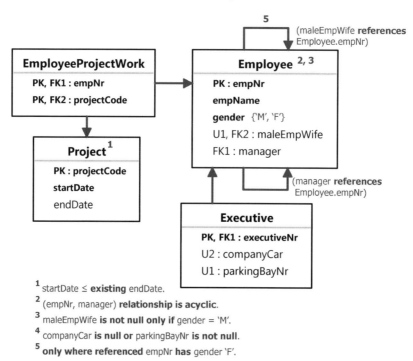

Figure 3.5   An annotated relational schema that captures further semantics

The value constraint on Gender is appended as {'M', 'F'} after the Employee.gender attribute. For clarification, I've annotated the foreign key references from the Employee table to identify the columns involved (NORMA displays these references as tooltips only when you hover the cursor over the arrows).

The rest of the annotations are provided by footnotes, with the footnote number placed next to the model element (a column, a table, or a foreign key reference). If the constraint applies to only one column, the footnote number appears as a superscript to the column. Figure 3.5 has no column footnotes, but as alternative to the {'M', 'F'} annotation you could apply the following footnote to the Employee.gender attribute: value in {'M', 'F'}.

If a constraint annotation involves more than one column in the same table, the footnote number appears as a superscript to the table name. Footnote 1 captures the ORM value-comparison constraint. For conceptual clarity, the keyword "existing" indicates that the constraint applies when a value exists for endDate, so if endDate is null the constraint is still satisfied. However, in SQL a constraint is violated only if it evaluates to False (not True and not Unknown), so in SQL this constraint is coded simply as the check clause: check(startDate <= endDate).

Footnote 2 captures the ORM acyclic const. Footnotes 3 and 5 enforce the ORM schema's subtyping restrictions on the roles of the MaleEmployee is husband of FemaleEmployee fact type. Footnote 4 captures the ORM subset constraint between the roles hosted by the Executive object type.

You can choose your own notation for such annotations. However, the annotated relational schemas provided at the end of the book in the Answers section basically follow the annotation style used here.

4 Modeling Exercises

This chapter includes several modeling exercises to consolidate your understanding of the ORM CSDP and further your practical experience with the NORMA tool for entering ORM schemas and mapping them to relational database schemas. Answers to all the exercises are provided in the Answers section at the back of the book.

4.1 Academic Conference

An information system is required to maintain details about academic events of two kinds (C = Conference, W = Workshop). An event that directly relies on another event that is a conference for its overall organization is said to be a satellite of that conference (which is called the host conference for the satellite event). Each event is chaired by at most three academics (the order in which these chairs are listed is not of interest).

The following report extract provides sample data of interest. A blank entry denotes an ordinary null. A "—" entry means "inapplicable because of some other entry".

Event	Kind	Duration (days)	Satellite of	Day held	Chair(s)
CAiSE2012	C	3		—	J. Krogstie, O. Pastor, B. Pernici
EMMSAD2012	C	2	CAiSE2012	—	T. Halpin, J. Krogstie, E. Proper
FBM2012	C	1		Monday	
ORM2012	W	3	OTM2012	—	H. Balsters, T. Halpin
DC2012	W	1	CAiSE2012	Saturday	
ABC2012	W	1		Monday	J. Smith
OTM2012	C	5		—	

Specify an ORM schema for this universe of discourse. Include relevant uniqueness, mandatory role, value, frequency and ring constraints, as well as definitions for derived subtypes. Omit implied ring constraints. Include an informal description for the fact type used to record satellite facts.

Use the NORMA tool to enter your ORM schema and map it to a relational schema. Annotate the relational schema to show all constraints and derivation rules. Also use the NORMA tool to generate a model report for the application.

4.2   Course Prerequisites

The following graph is extracted from a diagram that lists available courses as well as their (direct) prerequisites (if any). For example, course LG200 has no prerequisites, while course CS400 has two (direct) prerequisites. Each course has at most three (direct) prerequisites. Use the NORMA tool to specify an ORM schema for such a diagram. Include *uniqueness*, *frequency*, and *ring* constraints. Indicate whether an object type is *independent* (assuming no other facts about languages are of interest).

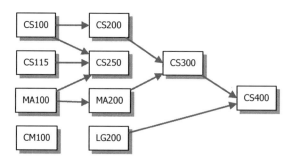

4.3   Concert Bookings

Part 1:

A concert-booking company books one-day concerts in various venues. It also handles all the ticket sales for these concerts, through its website. Each concert has one or more performers (artists or groups). Here is a small sample of relevant data (*Note*: The concert data are fictitious, although the performers named are real).

Concert	Performer(s)	Multi-act?	Date	Venue		
				Code	Name	Indoors?
C1	Donovan, Bob Dylan	Yes	30-10-2012	BEC	Brisbane Event Centre	Yes
C2 †	Wah!	No	30-10-2012	SBP	Southbank Park	No
C3	Bob Dylan, Donovan	Yes	15-12-2012	BEC	Brisbane Event Centre	Yes
C4	Wah!	No	22-12-2012	CCC	Caloundra Concert Centre	Yes
C5 †	Wah!	No	15-02-2013	MTH	Maleny Town Hall	Yes

† indicates that the concert is *free*

A multi-act concert has at least two such performers, and the order in which the performers are listed is not of interest. *Each combination of performer and date applies to only one concert. For a given date, at most one concert is at a given venue.* Each venue is identified by code but also has an identifying name. As the booking company and venues are in Australia, dates are displayed in day-month-year format.

For each **indoor** venue, seats are arranged in rows and columns, and each seat is either first class or second class. Here is a small sample of relevant data. The database includes such data for all indoor seats.

Seat			Seat
Venue	Row	Column	Class
BEC	A	1	1st
BEC	F	5	1st
BEC	Q	5	2nd
CCC	A	1	1st
CCC	F	5	2nd

*For each **indoor** concert that is **not free**,* tickets may be sold. Each ticket has a number that is globally unique over all concerts. Each ticket is good for one and only one particular seat at a particular concert. The class of a ticket (first or second class) is determined by the class of seat. Here is a small sample of relevant data.

Ticket Nr	Concert	Ticket Class	Seat Row	Seat Column
001345	C1	1st	A	1
001346	C1	1st	F	5
001347	C3	1st	A	1
001348	C4	2nd	F	5

Use the NORMA tool to specify an ORM conceptual schema for this UoD. Use *unary or binary fact types*, but do *not* use *n*-ary fact types.

Include all relevant *uniqueness* (internal or external), *mandatory role* (simple or disjunctive), *value, subset, equality* and *exclusion constraints*. For this exercise, do *not* use subtyping.

For each fact type that is derived, provide a derivation note to declare its derivation rule, and display this rule on the diagram using a model note.

Concert Bookings

Part 2:

Now suppose that the *order* in which performers are listed is of interest. For example, we want to know that in concert C1 Donovan performs first and Bob Dylan second, whereas in concert C3 they perform in the opposite order.

A sample report extract is shown below. Use the NORMA tool to remodel just this part of the domain using a *ternary fact type* to capture the order in which performers occur within concerts. For this question, include *uniqueness, mandatory role* and *value constraints*.

Your solution to Part 1 should have included a uniqueness constraint to ensure that on any given date, a performer performs for at most one concert. Make sure that your remodeled schema for Part 2 also includes a constraint to this effect.

Concert	Performer(s)
C1	Donovan Bob Dylan
C2	Wah!
C3	Bob Dylan Donovan
C4	Wah!
C5	Wah!

Concert Bookings

Part 3:

As an extension to the concert booking domain in Part 1, suppose that the fact type Venue has Nr1stClassSeats is added as a derived fact type to the ORM schema to compute the *number of first class seats* for each indoor venue.

Using other fact types in your solution to Part 1, specify a *derivation rule* for this fact type.

For this exercise, you need only write down the derivation rule. However, you are free to remodel the NORMA solution in this regard if you so wish.

4.4 British Monarchy

Part 1

An information system is needed to manage data about the British monarchy. For this exercise, you will design an ORM model to capture the information conveyed by the following reports. Data for these reports was extracted from various Web resources[1]. The following report lists basic details about all the monarchs.

Monarch	King	Queen	Age at death	Given Names
Anne		✓	49	Anne
George I	✓		67	George, Louis
George II	✓		76	George, Augustus
George III	✓		81	George, William, Frederick
George IV	✓		67	George, Augustus, Frederick
William IV	✓		71	William, Henry
Victoria		✓	81	Alexandrina, Victoria
Edward VII	✓		68	Albert, Edward
George V	✓		70	George, Frederick, Ernest, Albert
Edward VIII	✓		77	Edward, Albert, Christian, George, Andrew, Patrick, David
George VI	✓		56	Albert, Frederick, Arthur, George
Elizabeth II		✓		Elizabeth, Alexandra, Mary

The following report lists data about the house of each monarch. Owing to anti-German sentiment in the UK during World War I, the house of Saxe-Coburg and Gotha was replaced by the new house of Windsor when George V renamed his family name to "Windsor".

House	Monarchs		Replaced
	Count	Names	
Stuart	1	Anne	
Hanover	6	George I, George II, George III, George IV, William IV, Victoria	
Saxe-Coburg and Gotha	1	Edward VII	
Windsor	4	George V, Edward VIII, George VI, Elizabeth II	Saxe-Coburg and Gotha

---

[1] See, e.g., http://en.wikipedia.org/wiki/List_of_British_monarchs.

The following report lists data about births and deaths. Latitude and longitude are expressed in real numbers (for latitude, a positive number indicates degrees north, and negative indicates degrees south; for longitude, a positive number indicates degrees east, and negative indicates degrees west).

Treat the country location as asserted, even though in principle it could be derived from the grid reference.

Monarch	Birthdate	Birth						Died
		Birthplace						
		Name	Country		Grid reference			
			code	name	latitude	longitude		
Anne	1665 Feb 6	St James's Palace	GB	United Kingdom	51.504722	-0.1375		1714 Aug 1
George I	1660 May 28	Leineschloss	DE	Germany	52.370556	9.733611		1727 Jun 11
George II	1683 Oct 30	Herrenhausen	DE	Germany	52.403889	9.685556		1760 Oct 25
George III	1738 Jun 4	Norfolk House	GB	United Kingdom	51.507222	-0.133889		1820 Jan 29
George IV	1762 Aug 12	St James's Palace	GB	United Kingdom	51.504722	-0.1375		1830 Jun 26
William IV	1765 Aug 1	Buckingham Palace	GB	United Kingdom	51.501	-0.142		1837 Jun 20
Victoria	1819 May 24	Kensington Palace	GB	United Kingdom	51.505278	-0.188333		1901 Jan 22
Edward VII	1841 Nov 9	Buckingham Palace	GB	United Kingdom	51.501	-0.142		1910 May 6
George V	1865 Jun 3	Marlborough House	GB	United Kingdom	51.505	-0.135833		1936 Jan 20
Edward VIII	1894 Jun 23	White Lodge	GB	United Kingdom	51.4452	-0.2648		1972 May 28
George VI	1895 Dec 14	Sandringham House	GB	United Kingdom	52.829722	0.513889		1952 Feb 6
Elizabeth II	1926 Apr 21	Mayfair	GB	United Kingdom	51.508755	-0.14743		—

Use the NORMA tool to specify an ORM conceptual schema for this UoD, using one or two schema pages. Model the king and queen checkmark entries using two unary fact types. Include all relevant uniqueness constraints (internal or external) and mandatory role constraints (simple or disjunctive). Other constraints do apply, but ignore them for this part (some of these constraints are included in later parts of this exercise). If a fact type is derived, include it on the diagram as well as providing its derivation rule. You may ignore setting data types until Part 3 of the exercise.

British Monarchy

Part 2

The UoD is an expanded version of the British Monarchy domain discussed in Part 1. Use the ORM schema for Part 1 (available in the Answers section at the back of this book) as your starting point.

Add a constraint to ensure that if a monarch is dead, the date on which that monarch died is greater than or equal to the date on which that monarch was born.

The following report repeats some data from Part 1, but adds a column to record who is currently reigning. Strengthen the constraint between the king and queen predicates to ensure that each monarch is a king or queen but not both. Add an asserted fact type to record who is the reigning monarch, and add a constraint to ensure that this person cannot be dead. Also add a constraint to ensure that at most one monarch is reigning.

Monarch	King	Queen	Age at death	Reigning
Anne		✓	49	
George I	✓		67	
George II	✓		76	
George III	✓		81	
George IV	✓		67	
William IV	✓		71	
Victoria		✓	81	
Edward VII	✓		68	
George V	✓		70	
Edward VIII	✓		77	
George VI	✓		56	
Elizabeth II		✓		✓

The graph shown at the top of the next page displays the childhood relation among the British monarchs (e.g. Edward VIII and George VI are children of George V). Add a fact type to record this relation (no other parents or children are of interest), and apply all relevant constraints. Note that each monarch has at most one monarch as parent.

The following table about all countries is imported into the information system from a standard library of reusable models. To save space, only a small extract of this table is shown here. At most one former name may be recorded for any given country. Extend the model to cater for this information.

Childhood relations among British monarchs

Extract of country identifiers

CountryCode	CountryName	FormerName
AD	Andorra	
AE	United Arab Emirates	
AF	Afghanistan	
AG	Antigua and Barbuda	
...	...	...
LK	Sri Lanka	Ceylon
...	...	...
MM	Myanmar	Burma
...	...	...

For the reigning monarch, a list of all the countries over which he/she reigns as monarch is recorded, along with their population, if known, as shown in the next table. Here "?" indicates a null. Extend the model to cater for this information.

Note: The population figures were based on data available at the time of writing. For the latest population data for these and other countries, see a website such as https://en.wikipedia.org/wiki/List_of_countries_and_dependencies_by_population.

Reigning monarch	Country reigned over		
	Code	Name	Population
Elizabeth II	GB	United Kingdom	64,800,000
	CA	Canada	35,851,774
	AU	Australia	23,947,900
	PG	Papua New Guinea	7,398,500
	NZ	New Zealand	4,628,560
	JM	Jamaica	2,717,991

	SB	Solomon Islands	581,344
	BS	The Bahamas	368,390
	BZ	Belize	368,310
	BB	Barbados	285,000
	LC	St Lucia	185,000
	VC	St Vincent and the Grenadines	109,991
	GD	Grenada	103,328
	AG	Antigua and Barbuda	86,295
	KN	St Kitts and Nevis	?
	TV	Tuvalu	10,640

In this business domain, for each country that became a republic during the reign of a British monarch (thus ending the monarch's reign over that country), the year in which the country became a republic is recorded as well as the name of that monarch (who was therefore the last monarch to reign over that country). The following table shows the relevant data for the reigning monarch, but data for other republics and their last British monarch may also be included. Extend the model to cater for this information.

Monarch	Country over which the monarch was the last to reign		
	Code	Name	Year became a republic
Elizabeth II	LK	Sri Lanka	1972
	PK	Pakistan	1956
	ZA	South Africa	1961
...	...	...	...

Use the NORMA tool to specify an ORM conceptual schema for this UoD. *Include all relevant uniqueness, mandatory role, value-comparison, subset, exclusion, equality, ring, and role cardinality constraints*. If a fact type is *derived*, include it on the diagram as well as providing its *derivation rule*. Do NOT include any subtyping.

Note: Because subtyping is not allowed for this exercise, several set-comparison constraints (subset, exclusion or equality) are required to completely model this UoD.

British Monarchy

Part 3

The business domain is the British Monarchy domain described in Parts 1 and 2. An ORM schema solution for Part 2 is available for download as the NORMA file Monarchy2.orm at the following URL: http://1drv.ms/1NqCrbC. Download that file and use it as your starting point. The physical datatypes are mostly set to default datatypes, many of which need modification. Tasks are specified as follows.

1. Modify the ORM schema as follows.

Choose appropriate datatypes (including relevant facets such as length) for each value type. The easiest way to do this is to select the Object Types folder in the ORM Model Browser, then for each *value type* (depicted with a dashed line) make appropriate entries in its property grid. First choose the relevant DataType property. Assume that the Parts 1 and 2 data are representative.

For Text (Fixed Length or Variable Length), choose a Length (number of characters) big enough to hold the largest value. Store ages and years using numeric datatypes rather than temporal datatypes. NORMA converts the portable data types into the relevant physical data types for the chosen DBMS, but displays them in a common way in the Relational View (e.g. Text Variable Length displays as varchar in the relational view, but is mapped to nvarchar for Microsoft SQL Server). The following numeric ranges apply for Microsoft SQL Server.

tinyint	integer in the range 0 .. 255 (1 byte)
smallint	integer in the range -32,768 .. 32,767
integer	integer in the range -2,147,483,648 .. 2,147,483,647
bigint	integer in the range -2^{63} .. 2^{63}-1 (8 bytes)
decimal(p, s)	decimal number containing at most p digits, including s digits after the decimal point

Add informal descriptions for the following object types. To do this, select the object type and enter the explanation in its InformalDescription property. You may copy the note from the InformalDescription field or the Verbalizer into a documentation file in Microsoft Word or another word processor. The wording of the some of the following instructions assumes that Microsoft Word is the target word processor, but other word processors may be used instead.

House, CountryCode

Add an explanation of the following fact type (in its InformalDescription field), and copy it to a document in your word processor.

Monarch was last to reign over Country

Use the ORM Sample Population Editor to *add three rows of sample data to demonstrate that the fact type* Country has CountryName *is one-to-one.* Then select the fact type and copy all of its verbalization (including constraints and examples) to your Word document.

Save your revised model as Monarchy3.orm. Leave this model open while you perform task 2.

2. *Now map your conceptual schema to a relational schema.* To create the relational diagram (implemented as a view of the ORM schema), right-click in the document window, choose Extension Manager from the context menu, check Relational View in the dialog, and click the Relational View tab at the bottom of the Document window to display the relational diagram. Data types are displayed (you can suppress this display by toggling DisplayDataTypes in the property grid, but do not do so).

3. The automatically generated name for the table used to store the ternary fact type about given names is awkward. *Rename this fact type to match the table name you wish generated.* To rename a fact type, select the fact type in the ORM schema, and then edit its Name property.

4. The automatically generated names for several columns are awkward. *Add role names to relevant roles to generate some better column names.* To name a role, select it, and then enter the role name in its Name property. Make any *other column name changes* you wish using other name generation options discussed in chapter (e.g. excluding refmodes from column names) or by directly editing the column names on the relational view (e.g. for the house replacement columns).

5. In a couple of places, the automatically generated column order within tables is less than ideal. *Improve this order by dragging some columns to a better position in their table.*

6. Once you have finalized all the table and column names, *reposition the table shapes to produce a better layout.* Avoid edge crossing of foreign key constraint arrows.

7. Provide *partial documentation of the conceptual and logical models in a single document* in Microsoft Word as follows. Do *not* include the ORM a diagram.

    Open a Word document and copy the informal descriptions for the object types House, CountryCode and the fact type Monarch was last to reign over Country, as well as the verbalization including the sample population for the fact type Country has CountryName into the document as follows.

    To turn off hyperlinks when copying and pasting HTML verbalizations to Word, open the Tools/Options dialog, select the ORM Designer page, and open the dropdown for the Alternate Verbalization Text property in the Verbalization category. In the tree control, expand Core ORM Verbalization and Browser Settings. Double-click the checkbox beside Default, No Hyperlinks to choose the alternate verbalization. Now select the object type/fact type, select the relevant part(s) of its verbalization from the Verbalizer, copy it to the clipboard (press Ctrl+C), and paste it to Word (press Ctrl+V). You can later select the Default Verbalization setting to restore hyperlinks.

To turn off hyperlinks when copying and pasting HTML verbalizations to Word, open the Tools/Options dialog, select the 'ORM Designer' page, and open the dropdown for the 'Alternate Verbalization Text' property in the Verbalization category. In the tree control, expand 'Core ORM Verbalization' and 'Browser Settings'. Double-click the checkbox beside 'Default, No Hyperlinks' to choose the alternate verbalization. Now select the object type/fact type, select the relevant part(s) of its verbalization from the Verbalizer, copy it to the clipboard (press Ctrl+C), and paste it to Word (press Ctrl+V). You can later select the 'Default Verbalization' setting to restore hyperlinks.

Copy into the Word document the *verbalization of these four constraints:* (1) the exclusive-or constraint; (2) the equality constraint between two roles of Country; (3) the exclusion constraint between having died and reigning; and (4) the subset constraint. To do this, select the constraint, open the verbalizer, select the verbalization text, copy it to the clipboard (Ctrl+C), and paste the text to Word (Ctrl+V).

Copy the relational schema diagram (showing datatypes) into your Word document (Copy Image then Paste Special as Enhanced Metafile).

Annotate the relational schema to *display relational versions of all of the ORM graphic constraints and the two derived fact types.* For the derived attributes, indicate the relevant table to which it could be added as a computed column (for the derivation rules, simply use the derivation notes in the ORM schema).

4.5   Malaysia Database

Part 1

Malaysia is a federation of thirteen states and three federal territories. Eleven states and two territories are located in West Malaysia, on the Malay Peninsula. The other two states and one territory are located in East Malaysia on the island of Borneo (see below map).

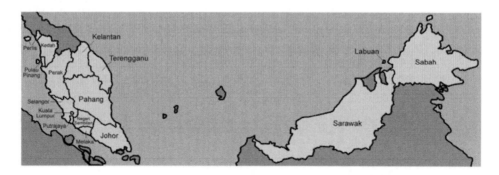

An information system is needed to manage data about Malaysia. For this first part of the exercise, you will design an ORM model to capture basic data as set out in the following reports. Data for these reports was extracted from various Web resources2.

The following table lists the name, abbreviation, and 2-letter ISO country code for the Malaysian states and federal territories. Use the abbreviation as the preferred reference scheme for a state or territory.

Name	Abbreviation	ISO code
Johor	JHR	MY-01
Kedah	KDH	MY-02
Kelantan	KTN	MY-03
Kuala Lumpur	KUL	MY-14
Labuan	LBN	MY-15
Melaka	MLK	MY-04
Negeri Sembilan	NSN	MY-05
Pahang	PHG	MY-06
Perak	PRK	MY-08
Perlis	PLS	MY-09
Pulau Pinang	PNG	MY-07
Putrajaya	PJY	MY-16
Sabah	SBH	MY-12
Selangor	SGR	MY-10
Sarawak	SWK	MY-13
Terengganu	TRG	MY-11

The following table shows additional data for the Malaysian states and federal territories3.

Abbrev.	Capital[4]	Region	Location	Status	Population	Area (km²)	Pop. density (/km²)
JHR	Johor Bahru	West	Malay Peninsula	State	3 300 000	19 984	165.1
KDH	Alor Setar	West	Malay Peninsula	State	1 818 188	9 426	192.9
KTN	Kota Bharu	West	Malay Peninsula	State	2 100 000	14 922	140.7
KUL	—	West	Malay Peninsula	Fed. Ter.	1 887 674	243	7768.2
LBN	Bandar Labuan	East	Borneo	Fed. Ter.	85 000	92	923.9
MLK	Bandar Melaka	West	Malay Peninsula	State	733 000	1 650	444.2
NSN	Seremban	West	Malay Peninsula	State	1 004 807	6 645	151.2
PHG	Kuantan	West	Malay Peninsula	State	1 396 500	25 964	53.8

---

[2] See, e.g., http://en.wikipedia.org/wiki/States_and_federal_territories_of_Malaysia

[3] The population data were accurate at the time I created the original version of this exercise, but will have changed a bit since then.

[4] i.e. the administrative capital

PRK	Ipoh	West	Malay Peninsula	State	2 260 576	21 006	107.6
PLS	Kangar	West	Malay Peninsula	State	215 000	810	265.4
PNG	George Town	West	Malay Peninsula	State	1 503 000	1 046	1436.9
PJY	—	West	Malay Peninsula	Fed. Ter.	50 000	46	1087.0
SBH	Kota Kinabalu	East	Borneo	State	3 387 880	76 115	44.5
SGR	Shah Alam	West	Malay Peninsula	State	5 000 000	7 956	628.4
SWK	Kuching	East	Borneo	State	2 500 000	124 450	20.1
TRG	Kuala Terengganu	West	Malay Peninsula	State	1 150 286	12 995	88.5

The following figures show additional data sheets for three states. Similar sheets are required for all eleven states. Each state has a unique combination of latitude and longitude. To cater for possible future changes to state borders, allow the same latitude to apply to more than one state, and allow the same longitude to apply to more than one state. For this part of the exercise, treat these data as applying directly to a state or territory (subtyping is delayed till Part 2).

The 3-part identification scheme (degrees, minutes, direction) for each coordinate should be modeled explicitly. A town or city is of interest if and only if it is the administrative or royal capital of a state. These towns/cities can be identified simply by their name. Some of these towns/cities have a secondary name (shown in parentheses after the standard name).

Negeri Sembilan

| Coordinates | 2° 45′ N |
| | 102° 15′ E |

Monarchy	Yes
Admin Capital	Seremban
Royal Capital	Seri Menanti

Ethnic Composition		Malay	Chinese	Indian	Other
	2000	57.9%	25.6%	16.0%	0.5%
	2005	54.96%	24.3%	15.18%	5.54%

Johor

| Coordinates | 1° 29′ N |
| | 103° 47′ E |

Monarchy	Yes
Admin Capital	Johor Baru
Royal Capital	Johor Baru

Ethnic Composition		Malay	Chinese	Indian	Other
	2000	57.1%	35.4%	6.9%	0.6%

Melaka				
Coordinates	2° 12' N 102° 15' E			
Monarchy Admin Capital Royal Capital	No Bandar Melaka (Malacca Town) —			
Ethnic Composition		Malay	Chinese	Indian	Other

	Malay	Chinese	Indian	Other
2000	63.8%	29.1%	6.5%	0.6%

Nine of the thirteen states are constitutional monarchies, and hence have royal capitals where the palace of official residence of the monarch is situated. A state's royal capital may be (but need not be) the same as its administrative capital.

The ethnic composition percentages are derived from population figures not shown here, and might not total 100% because of rounding to 1 or 2 decimal places. Treat all these percentages as simply asserted. For some states, no ethnic data might be available, while for others the ethnic data might be available for one or more years. You may assume that ethnic groups are confined to the four shown here. However, your model should allow ethnic data for other years (for any state) to be added when known.

Use the NORMA tool to specify an ORM conceptual schema for this UoD. Ignore the information provided by the initial map as to which states or territories border one another (this will be addressed in Part 2 of the exercise). Spread the schema over two pages, one for the first two tables, and one for the additional data sheets.

Include all relevant uniqueness and mandatory role constraints. Other constraints do apply, but ignore them for this part of the exercise. If a fact type is derived, include it on the diagram as well as providing its derivation rule. Subtyping does apply (e.g. the additional data on data sheets are recorded only for states), but ignore subtyping for this part of the exercise.

Malaysia Database
Part 2

The UoD is an expanded version of the Malaysia database domain from Part 1, except that town/city secondary names other than nicknames are no longer of interest. Use the ORM schema solution from Part 1 as your starting point. This schema is downloadable as the NORMA file Malaysia1.orm from the following URL: http://1drv.ms/1NBOR0A. Download and open the file, then delete the fact type TownOrCity has SecondaryName from this schema, as it is not required for Part 2.

Recall that Malaysia is a federation of thirteen states and three federal territories. Refine the model to ensure that only states (not federal territories) may be recorded to be a monarchy, and that only monarchies may have a royal capital. Also ensure that latitude/longitude and ethnic composition data are recorded only for states.

The UoD is extended to include cities or towns other than administrative or royal capitals. The population of each town and city mentioned in the information system must now be recorded, as well its state/territory and its rank based on the size of its population. The following table shows an excerpt from a related report which also contains some other details that need to be recorded. Cities are listed in **bold**, and towns are not. Here, an Em dash "—" means "inapplicable".

Rank	City/Town	State/Fed.Ter	Population	City status granted
1	**Kuala Lumpur**	Kuala Lumpur	1 458 790	1972-02-01
2	Subang Jaya	Selangor	1 174 972	—
3	Klang	Selangor	1 004 194	—
4	**Johor Baru**	Johor	867 507	1994-01-01
5	Ampang	Selangor	723 531	—
6	**Ipoh**	Perak	692 101	1988-05-27
7	**Kuching**	Sarawak	632 505	1988-08-01
8	**Shah Alam**	Selangor	577 626	2000-10-10
9	**Kota Kinabalu**	Sabah	543 765	2000-02-02
10	**Petaling Jaya**	Selangor	535 658	2006-06-20
11	Cheras	Selangor	460 699	—
12	Sandakan	Sabah	453 759	—
13	Seremban	Negeri Sembilan	405 674	—
...	...	...	...	...

Some cities have a main nickname, and also possibly a secondary nickname. The following table shows sample data. Here a double hyphen "--" simply means "not recorded" (e.g. because it is unknown or not existing).

City	Main Nickname	Secondary Nickname
Kuala Lumpur	KL	--
Johor Baru	JB	Bandar Raya Selatan
Ipoh	City of Millionaires	Bougainvillea City
Kuching	Cat City	--
Shah Alam	--	--
Kota Kinabalu	Nature Resort City	--
Petaling Jaya	PJ	Bandar Raya Inai Merah
...	...	...

For each federal territory, the year in which it was made a federal territory is recorded, as well as at most three of its tourist attractions. The following table provides the relevant data.

Federal Territory	Federated	Tourist attractions
Kuala Lumpur	1974	Aquaria KLCC
		Petrosains Discovery Centre
		National Planetarium
Labuan	1984	Labuan Bird Park
		Labuan water villages
Putrajaya	2001	--

Refer back to the map of Malaysia provided in Part 1. The information system is now required to list, for each state or territory, its neighboring states/territories (if any). Neighbors share a border on land. For example, Negeri Sembilan has Johor, Melaka, Pahang, Putrajaya, and Selangor as neighbors, but Labuan has no neighbors. Design the information system to minimize the data storage needed to provide such a list (use an asserted fact type to minimize the stored data, and a derived fact type to list each state/territory's neighbors in full).

Remodel the latitude and longitude aspects in the Malaysia1.orm schema to include precise value constraints for the three latitude components and the three longitude components (note that the possible directions and degrees differ). Also include value constraints for Status ('State', 'Fed.Ter'), Region, and EthnicGroup.

Use the NORMA tool to specify an ORM conceptual schema for this UoD. *Include all relevant uniqueness, mandatory role, value, subset, exclusion, equality, frequency, and ring constraints.* If a fact type is *derived*, include it on the diagram as well as providing its *derivation rule*. Include *subtyping*. If a subtype is derived rather than asserted, include a *derivation rule* for it. Where relevant, include *subtype constraints* (inclusive-or, exclusion, or exclusive-or) between subtype connections.

Include a constraint to ensure that each state must have an administrative capital (note that some but not all federal territories do have an administrative capital). *Hint*: A subset constraint may include a subtyping link as an argument (in this case, the supertype's role in the implicit, instance-level, identity relationship underlying the subtyping link is understood to be the argument).

Malaysia Database
Part 3

The UoD is the Malaysia database domain described in Parts 1 and 2. Use the ORM schema solution to Part 2 as your starting point. This schema is downloadable as the

NORMA file Malaysia2.orm from the following URL: http://1drv.ms/1O8JCIO. Download this conceptual schema. The physical data types are mostly set to default types, many of which need modification. Tasks are specified as follows.

1. Modify the ORM model as follows.

   Choose appropriate data types (including relevant facets such as length) for each value type. Assume that the Parts 1 and 2 data are representative. For Text (Fixed Length or Variable Length), choose a Length (number of characters) big enough to hold the largest value. For Numeric Decimal chose the Precision (total number of digits) and Scale (number of digits after the decimal point).

   Add informal descriptions for the following object types. To do this, select the object type and enter the explanation in its InformalDescription property. There is no need to create a ModelNote, as you may copy the note into Word from the InformalDescription field or the Verbalizer. Only basic notes are required.

   EthnicGroup, ISOcode, PopulationRank, StateOrTerritory

   Add an explanatory note to the following fact type (in its InformalDescription field). As you will copy this to a documentation glossary, you may delete the short model note for "X preborders Y" formerly provided on the diagram of the Part 2 solution.

   StateOrTerritory preborders StateOrTerritory

   Use the ORM Sample Population Editor to *add sample data to demonstrate that the preborders fact type is many-to-many*. Note: Ignore any error messages complaining that other constraints (e.g. mandatory role constraints) for StateOrTerritory are now violated.

   Save your revised model as Malaysia3.orm. Leave this model open while you perform task 2.

2. *Now map your conceptual schema to a relational schema.* To create the relational diagram, right-click in the Document window, choose Extension Manager from the context menu, check Relational View in the dialog, and click the Relational View tab at the bottom of the Document window to display the relational diagram.

   By default, NORMA uses the absorption option for mapping subtypes, so the functional fact types of State and Territory are absorbed into the StateOrTerritory table, and functional fact types of City are absorbed into the TownOrCity table. *Modify the property settings for the State and City subtypes* in the ORM schema to ensure that their functional fact types are instead grouped into *separate* State and City tables. Leave Territory absorbed.

3. The automatically generated names for tables and columns leave much to be de-sired. *Add names to each non-objectified m:n or n-ary fact type to match the table name you wish generated.* To rename a fact type, select the fact type, then edit its Name property.

4. *Add role names to relevant roles to help control how some column names are gen-erated.* To name a role, select it, and then enter the role name in its Name proper-ty. Make any *other column name changes* you wish using other name generation options (e.g. excluding refmodes from column names).

5. Once you have finalized all the table and column names, *reposition the table shapes to produce a better layout.* Try to avoid edge crossing of foreign key con-straint arrows. Where helpful, *reposition columns within their tables* by dragging them up or down directly on the relational view diagram.

6. Provide *partial documentation of the conceptual and logical models in a single Word* (or other word processor) *document* as follows.

    Copy the *informal descriptions for the object types* EthnicGroup, ISOcode, Population-Rank, and StateOrTerritory, *and the fact type* StateOrTerritory preborders StateOrTerritory, as well as the *sample population for this fact type* into the Word document as fol-lows. Select the object type/fact type, select the relevant part(s) of its verbaliza-tion from the Verbalizer, copy it to the clipboard (press Ctrl+C), and paste it to Word (press Ctrl+V). You may wish to modify the font.

    Copy into the Word document the *verbalization of these five constraints:* the pair-subset constraint from the admin capital fact type; the subset and exclusion constraints on nicknames; the simple frequency constraint; and the ring con-straint. To do this, select the constraint, open the verbalizer, select the verbaliza-tion text, copy it to the clipboard, and paste the text to Word.

7. Copy the *relational schema diagram (showing data types) into Visio or a Word document* (Copy Image then Paste Special as Enhanced Metafile), then *annotate the rela-tional schema diagram* to display relational versions of all the ORM constraints and derivation rules that are not displayed in NORMA's relational view. Use foot-noting for all the constraint annotations (including the value constraints).

    For a derivation rule that can be implemented as a derived attribute, indicate the relevant table to which it could be added as a computed column. Declare the derived borders relation as a view using any convenient notation.

4.6   Nobel Prize Awards

Part 1

The Nobel Foundation maintains a website at http://www.nobelprize.org/ that provides details on the annual *Nobel Prize awards*. Your task is to design a conceptual schema in ORM that is capable of storing most of the information available on this website.

You are encouraged to explore this website to familiarize yourself with the business domain. The website includes a form-based query facility for creating your own lists at http://www.nobelprize.org/nobel_prizes/lists/all/create.html.

A compact list of all the Nobel Prize awards is also accessible on Wikipedia's website at http://en.wikipedia.org/wiki/List_of_Nobel_laureates.

Starting in 1901, Nobel Prizes may be awarded annually for outstanding achievements in a given category. The following table lists the six Nobel categories and the awarding bodies that administer the awards in those categories. The Economic Sciences category was added in 1968.

Nobel Category	Awarding Body
Physics	The Royal Swedish Academy
Chemistry	The Royal Swedish Academy
Medicine or Physiology	The Nobel Assembly at Karolinska Institutet
Literature	The Swedish Academy
Peace	The Norwegian Nobel Committee
Economic Sciences	The Royal Swedish Academy

In each year in each category, a Nobel Prize may be awarded for one or two works (but not more than two works). On the Nobel website, a *work* is represented only by its *citation* (called "Prize motivation" in the create list query facility), e.g. "for the discovery of the accelerating expansion of the Universe through observations of distant supernovae".

However, for efficiency reasons we introduce *WorkNr* for the preferred identifier of a work.

Each work is by one, two or three *laureates*. A laureate (prize winner) is a person or organization. The following table shows a small extract of relevant data in this regard.

| Nobel Prize | | WorkNr | Laureate | Citation |
Year	Category			
...	...	...	...	...
2011	Physics	801	Saul Permutter Brian P. Schmidt Adam G. Riess	for the discovery of the accelerating expansion of the Universe through observations of distant supernovae
2011	Chemistry	802	Dan Shechtman	for the discovery of quasicrystals
2011	Medicine or Physiology	803	Bruce A. Beutler Jules A. Hoffman	for their discoveries concerning the activation of innate immunity
		804	Ralph M. Steinman	for his discovery of the dendritic cell and its role in adaptive immunity
2011	Literature	805	Thomas Tranströmer	because, through his condensed, translucent images, he gives us fresh access to reality
2011	Peace	806	Ellen Johnson Sirleaf Leymah Gbowee Tawakkol Karman	for their non-violent struggle for the safety of women and for women's rights to full participation in peace-building work
2011	Economic Sciences	807	Thomas J. Sargent Christopher A. Sims	for their empirical research on cause and effect in the macroeconomy
2010	Physics	794	Andre Geim Konstantin Novoselov	for groundbreaking experiments regarding the two-dimensiona;l material grapheme
...	...	...	...	...
2007	Peace	650	Intergovernmental Panel on Climate Change (IPCC)	for their efforts to build up and disseminate greater knowledge about man-made climate change, and to lay the foundations for the measures that are needed to counteract such change
...	...	...	...	...

A laureate may win many Nobel prizes over the years (in this exercise, a person or organization that wins more than one Nobel prize is treated as a single laureate). You may assume that a laureate may win many awards even in the same year (although the data does not illustrate this possibility).

If a work is by one or more persons, then for each person involved in that work a list is provided of the institutions (if any) with which that person was affiliated while doing the work. Each such institution (called a "Location" in the create list query facility) is identified simply by a name that may include a location, e.g. Australian National University (Canberra). The country in which each such institution is located is also stored. The following table shows some sample data in this regard.

WorkNr	Laureate	Affiliation	Country
801	Saul Permutter	Lawrence Berkeley National Laboratory (Berkeley, CA)	USA
		University of California (Berkeley, CA)	USA
	Brian P. Schmidt	Australian National University (Canberra)	Australia
	Adam G. Riess	John Hopkins University (Baltimore, MD)	USA
		Space Telescope Science Institute (Baltimore, MD)	USA

For each laureate that is an organization, the year in which it was founded is recorded, as indicated in the table extract below.

Laureate Organization	Founded
International Committee of the Red Cross	1863
Intergovernmental Panel on Climate Change (IPCC)	1988
United Nations (U.N.)	1945
...	...

For each laureate that is a person, details are recorded as in this table extract.

Laureate	Gender	Birth Country	Born	Died
Albert Einstein	M	Germany	1879	1955
Brian P. Schmidt	M	USA	1967	
Marie Curie	F	Poland	1867	1934
Saul Permutter	M	USA	1959	
...	...	...	...	...

If any two laureates are brothers of each other, this should be recorded (in both orderings) as indicated in the following table. For this exercise, assume that all brotherhood pairs are explicitly asserted, not derived. For example, if three persons are all brothers of one another then six brotherhood facts must be asserted to capture this information. *Note*: This might require more than one ring constraint shape.

Brother1	Brother2
Jan Tinbergen	Nikolaas Tinbergen
Nikolaas Tinbergen	Jan Tinbergen
...	...

Include the following ternary and unary derived fact types in your model, and provide derivation rules for them (a multiple winner is a laureate who won more than one Nobel prize).

> NobelCategory -prize in Year was awarded to Laureate.
> Laureate is a multiple-winner.

1. Use the NORMA tool to specify an ORM conceptual schema for this UoD. *Include all relevant graphical constraints*. If a subtype is *derived*, provide a *derivation rule for it*. Display all derivation rules in *model notes*, so they are visible on the schema diagram.

2. Suppose now that instead of exhaustively asserting brotherhood facts about brothers as above, we wish to minimize the number of such asserted facts and derive the others (e.g. if three persons are brothers of one another only two brotherhood facts need be asserted). Indicate in words or on a new diagram for just the brotherhood fact type how you would modify the constraints (textual and/or graphical) on the brotherhood fact type to best achieve this.

Nobel Prize Awards
Part 2

The business domain is the Nobel Prizes domain described in Part 1 Question 1. Use the ORM schema solution provided in the Answers and available as the NORMA file NobelPrize1.orm as your starting point. Download this file from the following URL: http://1drv.ms/1N0KJ7z. The physical data types are mostly set to default types, many of which need modification. Tasks are specified as follows.

1. *Modify the ORM model* as follows.

   Choose appropriate data types (including relevant facets such as length) for each value type. Assume that the Part 1 data are representative. For Text (Fixed Length or Variable Length), choose a Length (number of characters) to hold at least the largest value. For numeric data, choose unsigned small integer.

   Add informal descriptions for the following object types. To do this, select the object type and enter the explanation in its InformalDescription property. There is no need to create a ModelNote, as you may copy the note into Word from the InformalDescription field or the Verbalizer. Only basic notes are required.

Laureate, Work, LaureateWork

Add an explanatory note to the following fact type (in its InformalDescription field).

NobelCategory is administered by AwardingBody

Use the ORM Sample Population Editor to *add 2 or 3 rows of sample data* from Part 1 *to demonstrate that the administration fact type is many-to-one.*

Save your revised model as NobelPrize2.orm. Leave this model open while you perform the later tasks.

2. *Now map your conceptual schema to a relational schema* (ignoring the derived ternary). To create the relational diagram, right-click in the document window, choose Extension Manager from the context menu, check Relational View in the dialog, and click the Relational View tab at the bottom of the document window to display the relational diagram.

By default, NORMA uses the absorption option for mapping subtypes, so the functional fact types of Person and Organization are absorbed into the Laureate table.

Modify the AbsorptionChoice property setting for the Person and Organization subtypes in the ORM schema to ensure that their functional fact types are instead grouped into *separate* tables.

By default, NORMA does not generate columns or tables for derived fact types. Select the fact type Laureate is a multiple-winner and *change its DerivationStorage setting* to ensure that a relational column is generated to store facts of this kind. Leave the derived ternary fact type unchanged (currently, NORMA does not generate a relational construct for it).

3. Some automatically generated names for tables and columns are awkward. *Modify the names of each non-objectified m:n fact type to match the table name you wish generated.* To rename a fact type, select the ORM fact type, then edit its Name property.

Add role names to relevant roles to improve some of the generated column names. To name a role, select it, and then enter the role name in its Name property.

Make any *other column name changes* you wish using other name generation options (e.g. excluding refmodes from column names). You may also edit column names directly on the relational view.

4. Once you have finalized the table and column, *reposition the table shapes to produce a better layout*. Avoid edge crossing of foreign key constraint arrows. Reorder some columns in tables if you prefer a different order.

5. Provide *partial documentation of the conceptual and logical models in a Word or other word processor document* as follows.

   Copy the *informal descriptions for the object types* Laureate, Work, and Laureate-Work, *and the fact type* NobelCategory is administered by AwardingBody, as well as the *sample population for this fact type* into your document as follows. Select the object type/fact type, select the relevant part(s) of its verbalization from the Verbalizer, copy it to the clipboard (press Ctrl+C), and paste it to Word (press Ctrl+V).

   Copy into the Word document the *constraint verbalization of* the "≤ 2" frequency constraint, the external uniqueness constraint, the exclusive-or constraint, and the ring constraints. To do this, select the constraint, open the Verbalizer, select the verbalization text, copy it to the clipboard, and paste the text to your document.

6. Copy the *relational schema diagram (showing data types) into Visio or a Word document* (Copy Image then Paste Special as Enhanced Metafile), then *annotate the relational schema diagram* to display relational versions of all the ORM constraints and derivation rules that are not displayed in NORMA's relational view. (*Note:* To expose various modeling and mapping choices, the Person and Organization subtypes are asserted rather than derived).

   Use footnoting for all the constraint annotations (including the value constraints) as well as the rule for the stored and derived attribute for the multiple winner fact type. Declare the derived ternary relation as a view using any convenient notation.

4.7   Academy Awards

Part 1

Your task is to design an ORM conceptual schema for a database system that maintains information about the Academy Awards, as exemplified by the sample reports that follow.

Data for these reports have been extracted from various websites such as the following: http://en.wikipedia.org/wiki/Academy_Award and http://www.oscars.org/.

Starting in 1929, Academy Awards (called Oscars) have been awarded typically (but not always) once a year for outstanding achievements in a given category relating to motion pictures.

The following table is an extract from a report about all the Oscar ceremonies that either have been held (at the time of writing) or are already planned for the near future. The database system provides the current date (model this as the derived fact type Date is today). Each Oscar ceremony has at most six hosts.

For this exercise, assume that each ceremony is held in exactly one venue. A "—" mark means currently inapplicable, whereas "?" means currently unknown (ceremony hosts may be recorded before the ceremony).

Academy Award Ceremony

Nr	Date	Venue	Duration (minutes)	Hosts	Nr Hosts
1	1929-05-16	Hollywood Roosevelt Hotel	15	Douglas Fairbanks William C. deMille	2
2	1930-04-03	Ambassador Hotel	110	William C. deMille	1
3	1930-11-05	Ambassador Hotel	133	Conrad Nagel	1
...	...	...	...	...	...
11	1939-02-23	Biltmore Hotel	126	none	0
...	...	...	...	...	...
85	2013-02-24	Dolby Theatre	215	Seth McFarlane	1
86	2014-03-02	Dolby Theatre	214	Ellen DeGeneres	1
87	2015-02-22	Dolby Theatre	223	Neil Patrick Harris	1
88	2016-02-28	Dolby Theatre	—	?	?

For this database, Oscar nominees and winners are recorded only for past award ceremonies (held on a past date), and for just three categories of awards: Best Picture, Best Actor, and Best Actress. Duration and Oscar data for a past award ceremony may be entered any day after the ceremony, but when entered must be complete (i.e. the same data entry transaction must include the duration of the ceremony and the three Oscars awarded, as well as their nominees and winners).

Though not shown in these reports, each Oscar is primarily identified in the database by an auto-generated OscarId. The report extract at the top of the next page is from a list of the best picture nominees, with the winners listed first and in bold. For this exercise, assume that movies are identified simply by their name.

The second report extract on the next page lists the nominees and winners for the best actor and best actress awards, with the winner listed first in bold among the nominees. For each acting nomination each acting role (a character within a movie) used as a basis for that nomination is also listed. Though not shown in the sample data, it is possible for the same character name to appear in many movies.

Oscars for Best Picture Awards

| Award Ceremony | | Best Picture Nominees |
Nr	Date	(winner shown first)
1	1929-05-16	**Wings** Seventh Heaven The Racket
...	...	...
87	2015-02-22	**Birdman** American Sniper Boyhood The Grand Budapest Hotel The Imitation Game Selma The Theory of Everything Whiplash

Oscars for Best Actor and Best Actress Awards

| Oscar | | Nominees | Acting Role | |
Ceremony Nr	Category		Movie	Character Played
1	Best Actor	**Emil Jannings** Richard Barthelmess	The Last Command The Way of All Flesh The Noose The Patent Leather Kid	Sergius Alexander August Schilling Nickie Elkins patent leather kid
	Best Actress	**Janet Gaynor** Louise Dresser Gloria Swanson	Seventh Heaven Street Angel Sunrise: A Song of two Humans A Ship Comes In Sadie Thompson	Diane Angela The Wife Mrs Pleznik Sadie Thompson
...	...	...	...	...
62	Best Actor	**Daniel Day-Lewis** Morgan Freeman ...	My Left Foot Driving Miss Daisy ...	Christy Brown Hoke Colburn ...
	Best Actress	**Jessica Tandy** Jessica Lange ...	Driving Miss Daisy Music Box ...	Daisy Werthan Ann Talbot ...
...	...	...	...	...
87	Best Actor	**Eddie Redmayne** Steve Carell ...	The Theory of Everything Foxcatcher ...	Stephen Hawking John du Pont ...
	Best Actress	**Julianne Moore** Marion Cotillard ...	Still Alice Two Days, One Night ...	Alice Howland Jane Hawking ...

Each movie is nominated for best picture or stars someone nominated for Best Actor or Best Actress. Details for movies are recorded as shown in the following report extract (to save space, only a small selection of movies is listed here). Though rare, it is possible that a movie has more than one director (e.g. the Coen brothers directed the movie titled 'No Country for Old Men'). Though not shown in our sample data, it is also possible for the same person to direct many movies.

Movies

Movie	Director(s)	Duration (minutes)	Vocality	Spoken Language
Amour	Michael Haneke	127	vocal	French
A Ship Comes In	William K. Howard	70	silent	—
Birdman	Alejandro G. Inarritu	119	vocal	English
No Country for Old Men	Ethan Coen, Joel Coen	122	vocal	English
Wings	William A. Wellman	141	vocal	English
...	...	...	...	...

If the father of an acting nominee is also an acting nominee, this is recorded, as indicated below.

Fatherhood among acting nominees

Father	Child
Henry Fonda	Jane Fonda
Henry Fonda	Peter Fonda
...	...

Use the NORMA tool to specify an ORM conceptual schema for this UoD. *Include all relevant graphical constraints.* If a fact type or subtype is *derived*, provide a *derivation rule for it*, and enter this as a DerivationNote property (so an asterisk is displayed on the diagram). Also, display all derivation rules in *model notes*, so they are visible on the schema diagram. For the Date is today fact type, your derivation note should simply state that it is system derived.

Academy Awards
Part 2

The business domain is the Academy Awards domain described in Part 1. Use the ORM schema solution to Part 1 provided in the Answers as your starting point. This schema is available as the NORMA file AcademyAward.orm which you may download from the following URL: http://1drv.ms/1P5cba4. The physical data types in this file are mostly set to default types, many of which need modification. Tasks are specified as follows.

1. *Modify the ORM model* as follows.

   Choose appropriate data types (including relevant facets such as length) for each value type. First choose the relevant DataType property. Assume that the Part 1 data are representative. For Text (Fixed Length or Variable Length), choose a Length (number of characters) to hold at least the largest value. For numeric data other than OscarId, choose unsigned small integer.

   Add informal descriptions for the following object types. To do this, select the object type and enter the explanation in its InformalDescription property. There is no need to create a ModelNote, as you may copy the note into Word from the InformalDescription field or the Verbalizer. Only basic notes are required.

   > ActingRole, Vocality

   Add an explanatory note to the following fact type (in its InformalDescription field).
   > OscarCeremony is hosted by Person

   Use the ORM Sample Population Editor to *add 3 rows of sample data* from Part 1 *to illustrate that the* OscarCeremony is held at Venue *is many-to-one.* You may ignore model errors caused by not populating the other mandatory roles for OscarCeremony (if you wish to remove those errors, populate those fact types too).

   Save your revised model as AcademyAward2.orm. Leave this model open while you perform the later tasks.

2. *Now map your conceptual schema to a relational schema.* To create a basic relational diagram, right-click in the document window, choose Extension Manager from the context menu, check Relational View in the dialog, and click the Relational View tab at the bottom of the document window to display the relational diagram. Data types are displayed.

   By default, NORMA uses the absorption option for mapping subtypes, so the functional fact types of subtypes are absorbed into their supertype table. *Modify the AbsorptionChoice property setting for the BestPictureOscar and ActingOscar subtypes* in the ORM schema to ensure that their functional fact types are instead grouped into *separate* tables. By default, NORMA does not generate columns or tables for derived fact types.

3. Some automatically generated names for tables and columns are awkward. *Modify the names of each non-objectified m:n fact type to match the table name you*

wish generated. To rename a fact type, select the ORM fact type, and then edit its Name property. *Add role names to relevant roles to improve some of the generated column names.* To name a role, select it, and then enter the role name in its Name property. Make any *other column name changes* you wish by editing column names directly on the relational view—you may also use other name generation options discussed earlier (e.g. excluding refmodes from column names).

4. Once you have finalized the table and column names, *reposition the table shapes to produce a better layout.* Try to avoid edge crossing of foreign key constraint arrows. *Reorder some columns* in tables if you prefer a different order.

5. Provide *partial documentation of the conceptual and logical models in a single Word document* as follows.

   Copy the *informal descriptions for the object types* ActingRole and Vocality, *and the fact type* OscarCeremony is hosted by Person, as well as the verbalization and *sample population for the fact type* OscarCeremony is held at Venue into the Word document as follows. Select the object type/fact type, select the relevant part(s) of its verbalization from the Verbalizer, copy it to the clipboard (press Ctrl+C), and paste it to Word (press Ctrl+V). You may wish to modify the font.

   To *turn off hyperlinks when copying and pasting HTML verbalizations to Word,* open the Tools/Options dialog, select the ORM Designer page, and open the dropdown for the Alternate Verbalization Text property in the Verbalization category. In the tree control, expand Core ORM Verbalization and Browser Settings. Double-click the checkbox beside Default, No Hyperlinks to choose the alternate verbalization. Now select the object type/fact type, select the relevant part(s) of its verbalization from the Verbalizer, copy it to the clipboard and paste it to Word. You can later select the Default Verbalization setting to restore hyperlinks.

   Copy into the Word document the *constraint verbalization of* the "≤ 6" frequency constraint, the equality constraint, the subset constraint between the best picture winner and nominee fact types, and the ring constraint. To do this, select the constraint, open the Verbalizer, select the verbalization text, copy it to the clipboard, and paste the text to Word.

6. Copy the *relational schema diagram (showing data types) into Visio or your word processor* (Copy Image then Paste Special as Enhanced Metafile), then *annotate the relational schema diagram* to display relational versions of all the ORM constraints and derivation rules that are not displayed in NORMA's relational view (except you may ignore the derivation rule for Date is today, since the current date is provided by the DBMS system itself). Use footnoting for the bulk of these additional constraints and derivation rules.

5 Transforming and Optimizing Schemas

This chapter discusses some of the main ways of transforming ORM schemas into alternative but equivalent schemas, and provides guidelines for choosing such transformations in order to optimize or improve the efficiency of the relational schema generated from the ORM schema via the Rmap procedure. It also includes exercises to consolidate the ideas discussed. Exercise answers are in the back of the book.

5.1 Conceptual Schema Transformations

Basically, two schemas are *semantically equivalent* if and only if each UoD state or transition that can be modeled in one schema can also be modeled in the other. Intuitively, most people would regard the ORM schemas in Figure 5.1 to be equivalent in this way. Given that the relational attributes isMale and isFemale are *Boolean*, most would also treat the mapped relational schemas (c) and (d) as equivalent.

More strictly, formal equivalence of these ORM schemas requires that we include Gender and its reference scheme as 'virtual types' in ORM schema (a), and conservatively extend the schemas with derivation rules so each schema can derive predicates in the other schema. For example, ORM schema (a) is extended with the rule Person has Gender **iff** Person is male **and** (Gender has GenderCode 'M' **or** Person is female and Gender has GenderCode 'F'), and ORM schema (b) is extended with the rules Person is male **iff** Person has Gender 'M' and Person is female **iff** Person has Gender 'F'. With such extensions, the schemas can be proven to be logically equivalent using classical logic. From this point onwards, our discussion of schema transformations will ignore such formal extensions.

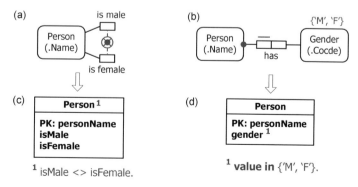

Figure 5.1   Equivalent ORM schemas may map to different relational schemas

ORM includes many *schema transformation* theorems that enable an ORM schema to be transformed into another ORM schema that is either equivalent to it or implied by it. In this section, we briefly discuss some of the more useful kinds of equivalence transformations. In the next section, we provide guidelines for performing such transformations prior to relational mapping in order to generate a more efficient relational schema. As a trivial example, the relational schema (d) in Figure 5.1 might be slightly preferable to the relational schema (c) Figure 5.1.

In Figure 5.1, the transformation of ORM schema (a) into ORM schema (b) is case of *predicate generalization*, since the is male and is female predicates are generalized into a single hasGender predicate that covers both of the original cases. The transformation in the opposite direction is known as *predicate specialization*. Figure 5.2 provides another example, this time transforming a single ternary fact type into three binaries. In both Figure 5.1 and Figure 5.2, the generalized fact type includes an object type that is outside the scope of the internal uniqueness constraint but is subject to an enumerated value constraint. This is the most common kind of case for predicate specialization.

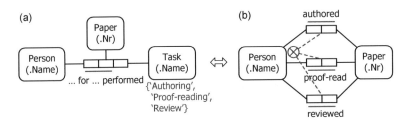

Figure 5.2   Another example of predicate specialization/generalization

If the object type with the value constraint lies within the scope of the internal uniqueness constraint, the specialization transformation does not generate an exclusion constraint, but it does shorten the uniqueness constraint. Figure 5.3 provides a simple example.

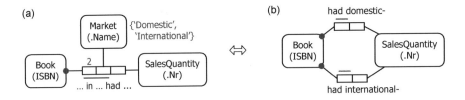

Figure 5.3   Yet another case of predicate specialization/generalization

In a third kind of predicate specialization/generalization transformation, an object type with a value constraint may be absorbed into another fact type to specialize it into multiple fact types, one for each of its values. Figure 5.4 provides an example.

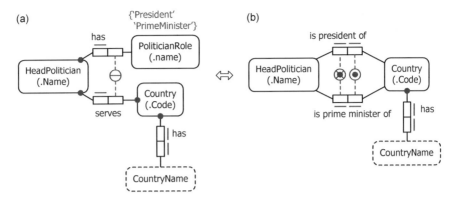

Figure 5.4   A further case of predicate specialization/generalization

Other kinds of specialization/generalization transforms do exist, but they are not as common as the three cases we have just considered, so are not elaborated on here (although the section exercise includes some examples). A detailed coverage of all of ORM's specialization/generalization theorems and their corollaries may be found in section 14.2 of Halpin & Morgan (2008).

Another class of schema transformations allows conversion between nested, co-referenced and flattened styles. As an example, suppose we need to provide an ORM schema to capture the grades obtained by students in courses at the end of the current semester. A small extract of sample data is shown in Table 5.1. Figure 5.5 shows three ways to schematize this report.

Table 5.1   Extract of a report showing the grades obtained by students in courses

StudentNr	Course	Grade
101	CS100	A
101	MA100	B
102	CS100	A

Figure 5.5   Modeling Table 5.1 by (a) flattening, (b) coreferencing, and (c) nesting

The schema in Figure 5.5(a) models the report using a single fact type. This is called a *flattened* approach. The schema in Figure 5.5(b) models the report using Enrollment as a coreferenced entity type (each enrolment is identified by a combination of course and student). This is called a *coreferenced* approach.

The schema in Figure 5.5(c) models the report by *objectifying* the enrollment fact type as Enrollment, and then attaching the grade result to it. This is called a *nested* approach, as you can visualize the enrolment fact type as nested inside the Enrollment object type.

Now let's modify our example to allow that some grade results for the semester are not yet known. For example, if the final exam for course MA100 has not yet been held, we may know that student 101 enrolled in MA100, but his/her grade is currently unknown. Table 5.2 indicates using "?" as a null entry.

Table 5.2   Modified report extract where some grades may be unknown

StudentNr	Course	Grade
101	CS100	A
101	MA100	?
102	CS100	A

Figure 5.6(a) models this report using a flattened approach, In this case, two fact types are needed, one for recording the enrollment information, and one for the recording the grade resulting from that enrollment, if known. The pair-subset constraint ensures that if a student scored a grade for a course then he/she must have enrolled in that course. Figure 5.6(b) and Figure 5.6(c) show the coreferenced and nested versions. The Enrollment type is declared independent (see appended "!") and its grade result role is now optional.

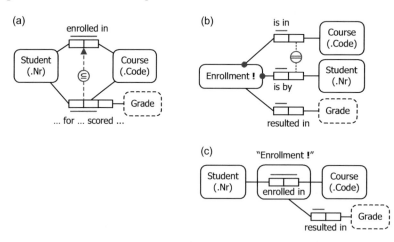

Figure 5.6   Modeling Table 5.2 by (a) flattening, (b) coreferencing, and (c) nesting

The flattened version of the ORM schema shown in Figure 5.6(a) relationally maps to two tables, with the pair-subset constraint captured by a composite foreign key reference, as shown in Figure 5.7(b). Currently, NORMA does not generate the foreign key reference, so its relational view displays simply as shown in Figure 5.7(a). This known bug should eventually be fixed in a later version of NORMA.

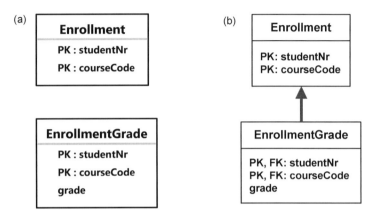

Figure 5.7   Relational schema mapped from the flattened enrollment schema

In contrast, both the coreferenced and nested versions of the enrollment schema in Figure 5.6 relationally map to a single Enrollment table, with grade as an optional attribute, as shown in Figure 5.8. This relational schema is typically much more efficient than the two table relational schema generated from the flattened ORM schema. Hence, ORM recommends transforming this kind of flattened schema into either a coreferenced or nested version before invoking the Rmap procedure.

In Figure 5.6(a) the (Student, Course) role pairs in the two fact types are related by a subset constraint. This is by far the most common situation in which a nesting or coreferencing transform is typically desirable. However, a nesting or coreferencing transformation can still be taken if the compatible role sequences in the fact types are related by an equality or exclusion constraint or even by no constraint. For a detailed discussion of ORM's overlap algorithm that handles such cases, see section 14.3 of Halpin & Morgan (2008).

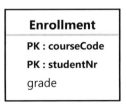

Figure 5.8   Relational map from the coreferenced and nested enrollment schemas

Yet another class of schema transformations involves *role reduction*, where a role is either eliminated from an ORM schema (*role elimination*) or is redirected to a different predicate (*role redirection*). As an example of role elimination, consider the report extract about countries and their politicians shown in Table 5.3.

Table 5.3   Extract from a report listing countries and their politicians

Country	Politician	is Head Politician
AU	Malcom Turnbull	True
	Julie Bishop	False
	Penny Wong	False
	...	...
US	Barack Obama	True
	Joe Biden	False
	Hillary Clinton	False
	...	...
...	...	...

Figure 5.9(a) shows one way to model Table 5.3, with its relational map shown in Table 5.3(c). The countryHeaded attribute is nullable, so its uniqueness constraint is understood to apply only to non-null entries. The annotated relational constraint in Figure 5.9(c) captures the ORM pair-subset constraint.

Figure 5.9(b) shows the ORM schema obtained by applying a role elimination transform to the ORM schema in Figure 5.9(a). The binary heads predicate has been reduced to a unary predicate. The external uniqueness constraint involves a unary, so is a unique-where-true constraint, and is captured by the annotation in the relational schema shown in Figure 5.9(d), where the isaHeadPolitician attribute is Boolean.

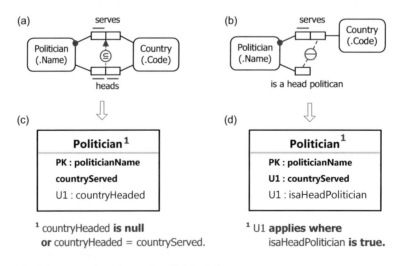

Figure 5.9   Two ways to schematize Table 5.3

The attribute isaHeadPolitician should be non-nullable, but currently NORMA does not assume closed world semantics for unaries, so does not display this attribute in bold type. Support for choice of world assumption status (closed world, open world, or open world with negation) for unaries is planned for a later release of NORMA.

In Figure 5.9(d), the attribute name "isaHeadPolitician" is used as shorthand for "is head politician of the country served". Clarification of this meaning should be provided in a term glossary.

Intuitively, most users would prefer the relational schema in Figure 5.9(d) over that of Figure 5.9(c), especially when the tables are populated with data, since the non-null entries for countryHeaded would always match that of countryServed.

Now consider the ORM schema shown in Figure 5.10. The subset constraint ensures that each main city that is the capital of a country must also be located in that country. The relational schema to which this ORM schema maps is shown at the bottom of Figure 5.10. To save space, this is specified in my "horizontal notation" for relational schemas rather than as an annotated version of the relational view diagram generated by NORMA.

Here, keys are underlined. If a table scheme has multiple keys, the primary key is doubly-underlined. Subset constraints are depicted by arrows from source to target. The arrow from Country.(capitalCountryCode, capitalCityName) to MainCity.countryCode denotes a foreign key reference, as does the downward arrow from MainCity.countryCode to Country.countryCode. The upward arrow from Country.countryCode to MainCity.countryCode is a subset constraint (but not a foreign key reference).

The "=" operator linking Country.countryCode and Country.capitalContryCode means their entries must match. This constraint would typically be implicitly assumed by users.

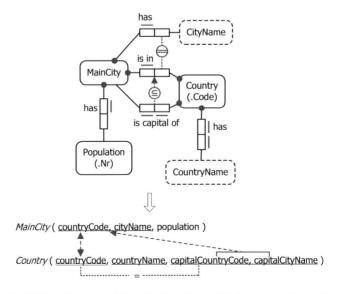

Figure 5.10   An ORM schema and its relational map (in horizontal notation)

This repetition of the same country code can be avoided, and the relational schema simplified, by first applying a *role redirection* transform to the ORM schema. In Figure 5.11, the ORM schema has redirected Country's capital role from MainCity to CityName. As you can see from the relational map, this reduces the Country table to just three columns, and simplifies the overall constraint enforcement.

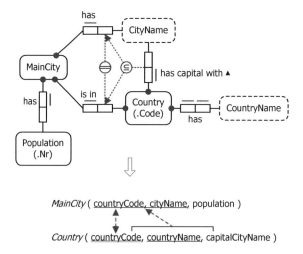

Figure 5.11   The result of applying a role redirection transform to Figure 5.10

Some further though less common classes of schema transformation are discussed in Halpin & Morgan (2008), along with a more detailed discussion of role elimination transforms. For a much more detailed account of both role elimination and role redirection transforms, see Halpin, Carver & Owen (2007).

Exercise 5.1

1. Apply *predicate specialization* transformations to the following ORM schemas. The transformations for schemas (b) and (d) are based on the frequency constraint (this flavor of predicate specialization was not discussed earlier, but should hopefully be obvious).

    (a)

    (b)

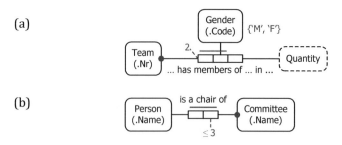

(c)

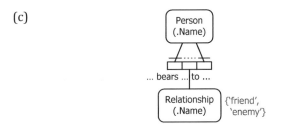

(d)

2. Apply *predicate generalization* to the following ORM schema.

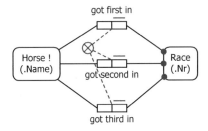

3. (a)   Apply *nesting* to the following ORM schema.

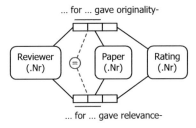

   (b)   Apply *co-referencing* to your solution.

4. Use *role elimination* to transform the ORM schema shown opposite into one that will result in a more efficient relational schema.

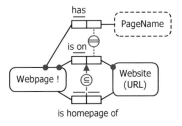

5. Use *role redirection to* transform the ORM schema shown below.

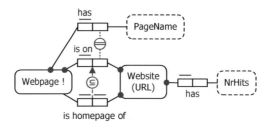

5.2   Conceptual Schema Optimization

Conceptual schema optimization is the process of transforming a conceptual schema into an alternative conceptual schema that maps to a more efficient implementation schema in the target system. In this book, we assume that the conceptual schema is an ORM schema and that the target system is a relational DBMS.

The optimization is usually designed to improve the execution speed of typical *queries* and/or typical *updates*, but might also be used simply to improve the *clarity* of the relational schema.

Overall, the optimization procedure comprises five main steps which are arranged in the following three main stages:

- Transform to reduce the number of mapped tables (steps 1 and 2).
- Transform to simplify individual tables (steps 3–5).
- Where applicable, apply role reduction transforms.

As discussed earlier, different options exist for mapping functional roles on subtypes. Subtype mapping choices should be made before applying the optimization procedure discussed in this section. By default, NORMA chooses absorption rather than separation, as this reduces the number of tables. Steps 1 and 2 of the optimization procedure also aim to *reduce the number of tables*.

Poorly performing queries usually involve joins or subqueries, and reducing the number of tables tends to minimize the need for joins or subqueries. Updates that require checking constraints between tables also tend to be expensive, so the table reduction strategy can often improve update performance as well.

Figure 5.12 summarizes step 1 of the conceptual schema optimization procedure. Step 1.1 covers a rare case where flattening is preferred over nesting, and then applies predicate specialization to long predicates. Step 1.2 applies predicate generalization to mutually exclusive predicates. Step 1.3 then applies a nesting or coreferencing transform to a pair of fact types whose composite keys are compatible.

1.1   Flatten each objectified predicate that hosts just a single, mandatory role,
e.g.

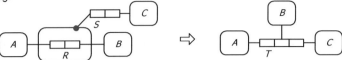

If another compatible, composite key can be formed by absorbing a low cardinality object
type into a predicate with a key of arity ≥ 3 then do so,
e.g.

1.2   If n nonfunctional, whole predicates form compatible, composite, exclusive keys and are
incompatible with all other (sub-)predicates then generalize them into a single longer
predicate by extracting an object type of cardinality n,
e.g.

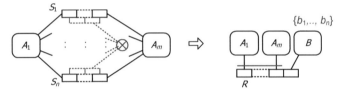

1.3   Apply the overlap algorithm to each pattern of compatible, composite keys,
e.g.

Figure 5.12   Optimization step 1: unify compatible, composite keys

Step 2 of the optimization procedure considers *object types with both a functional*
(simple uniqueness constraint) *role and a nonfunctional role*, and typically attempts
to replace the nonfunctional role by functional roles that can be grouped into the
same table as the original functional role. The overall step is divided into two stages,
as summarized in Figure 5.13 on the following page.

Most of step 2.1 applies predicate specialization by absorbing a value constrained object type or creating individual cases for a frequency constraint. Step 2.2
also applies predicate specialization, although the cases considered here are fairly
rare. As an example of the final part of step 2.2, the head politician schema considered earlier in Figure 5.4(a) is transformed into the schema in Figure 5.4(b). In this
case, HeadPolitician is the object type B, and its functional roles in Figure 5.4(a) are
mandatory so an equality constraint between them is implied. The schema in Figure
5.4(a) maps to two tables, whereas the Figure 5.4(b) schema maps to a single table.

2.1

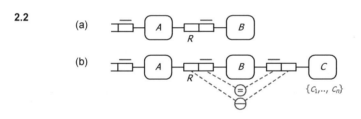

For each case where an object type *A* has simple and binary keys attached,
where the other role of the binary key is hosted by *B*:
if *R* is a binary predicate
then if *B* has values $b_1,..., b_n$ (and *n* is small)
    then specialize *R* to *n* unaries **or** replace *B* by *B'* {b_1, b_2, both} (if *n* = 2)
      making the key(s) simple
    else if *A*'s role in *R* has a frequency constraint *n* or *n* (and *n* is small)
      then specialize *R* into *n* exclusive binaries simply keyed on *A*
      else if *A* has just one functional role
        and the predicates are compatible, pair-exclusive binaries
        then generalize both to a single ternary with a restricted uniqueness constraint
else -- *R* is a ternary
    if *B* has values $b_1,.., b_n$ (and *n* is small)
    then absorb *B*, specializing *R* into *n* binaries simply keyed on *A*.

2.2

(a) [diagram]

(b) [diagram] {$c_1,.., c_n$}

For each case where an object type *A* has a functional role attached, as well as a 1:*n* binary
predicate *R* connected to object type *B*:
if *B* has no other functional roles -- case (a) above
then if *A*'s role in *R* has a frequency constraint of *n*, or *n* (and *n* is small)
    then specialize *R* into *n* 1:1 binaries with *B*'s roles mutually exclusive
    else if *B* has values $b_1,.., b_n$ (and *n* is small)
      then consider specializing *R* into *n* unaries
else if *B* has exactly one more functional predicate, linked to *C* {$c_1,.., c_n$}
    and an equality constraint spans *B*'s functional roles
    and an external uniqueness constraint spans *B*'s co-roles -- case (b) above
    then specialize *R* into *n* 1:1 binaries with *B*'s roles exclusive, by absorbing *C*.

Figure 5.13   Optimization step 2

To illustrate how steps 1 and 2 of the optimization procedure can reduce the number of tables generated in relational mapping, consider the ORM schema shown in Figure 5.14. Recall that the Rmap algorithm maps fact types with composite uniqueness constraints to separate tables, while functional fact types attached to an object type are grouped into a table keyed on that object type. As an optional exercise, determine how many relational tables this maps to before reading on.

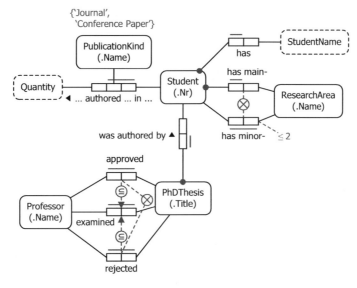

Figure 5.14 **This schema maps to seven tables**

The five fact types with composite keys map to their own tables. The two functional fact types of Student map to a Student table, and authorship fact type for PhDThesis maps to a PhDThesis table. So we obtain seven tables, as shown in Figure 5.15. To save space, the relational schema is displayed in horizontal notation. The dashed arrows denote foreign key constraints. Constraint arguments spanning multiple attributes are connected by a linking line. The value constraint and frequency constraint are placed next to the relevant attribute. The exclusion constraints are depicted with a circled cross.

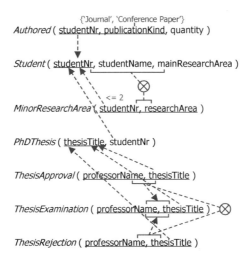

Figure 5.15 **The relational schema mapped from Figure 5.14**

Applying steps 1 and 2 of the conceptual schema optimization procedure leads to an ORM schema such as that shown in Figure 5.16. Some role names have been added to finesse the names of the relational columns generated by NORMA.

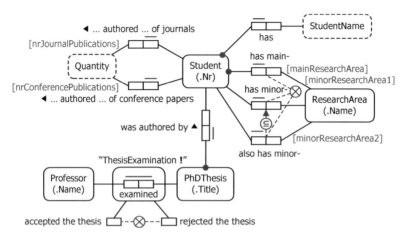

Figure 5.16   The ORM schema after optimizing the ORM schema in Figure 5.14

Predicate specialization was used to transform the fact types Student authored PublicationKind in Quantity and Student has minor ResearchArea. Though not required, I decided to order the minor research topics for each student, so I added the pair-subset constraint shown. These transformed fact types all have functional roles attached to Student, so may be grouped into the Student table.

I used nesting to transform the three fact types relating professors to PhD theses, thus reducing three former relational tables to one. The optimized relational schema now has three tables instead of seven, as shown in Figure 5.17, and the constraint enforcement pattern is considerably simplified compared with that of Figure 5.15.

The horizontal notation for relational schemas encloses nullable columns in square brackets. Nesting of square brackets indicates that the inner-bracketed attribute can have a non-null value only if the outer-bracketed value on the same row is non null. An inequality operator "≠" connected by dashed lines to multiple attributes means that non-null values of these attributes on the same row must differ.

Figure 5.17   The optimized relational schema mapped from Figure 5.16

3

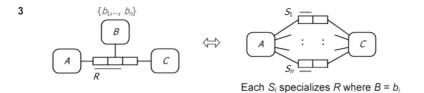

Each S_i specializes R where $B = b_i$

For the ternary pattern shown, if important queries or derivations on R require
comparisons between different tuples, and the values $b_1,..., b_n$ are few and fairly stable,
then absorb B, specializing R into n functional binaries.

Figure 5.18   Optimization step 3: the Table Width Guideline

Step 3 of the conceptual schema optimization procedure is set out in Figure 5.18.
rather than reducing the number of tables, it aims to reduce self-joins in queries on a
single table. It is called the *Table Width Guideline*, since it indicates when a wider table (with more columns) might be preferred.

If the object type B hosts a functional role in an elementary fact type, the predicate specialization transform by absorbing B will have already been carried out in
step 2.1. Otherwise, step 3 now invokes the predicate specialization.

As an example, Table 5.4 shows an extract of country population data for 2014
and 2015. To save space, figures are shown for only China and the USA. For full data,
see http://statisticstimes.com/population/countries-by-population.php. For this
business domain, the only years of interest are 2014 and 2015.

Table 5.4   Extract from a report listing country populations in 2014 and 2015

Country	Year	Population	Change
CN	2014	1,393,783,836	
	2015	1,401,586,609	7,802,773
US	2014	322,583,006	
	2015	325,127,634	2,544,628
...	...	...	

For each country, the population change figure can be derived by subtracting the
population in 2014 from the population in 2015. However, the way in which this
derivation (or query) is specified depends on how we structure the asserted fact
types. Two ways to schematize the asserted facts are shown in Figure 5.19.

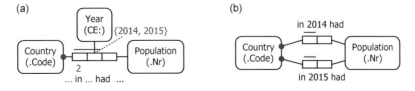

Figure 5.19   Two ways of modeling the asserted facts in Table 5.4

$$\overset{2}{}\quad \overset{\{2014,\,2015\}}{}$$

PopulationData (<u>countryCode, censusYear</u>, population)

SQL code for query to derive the population change:

select *Old*.countryCode, *New*.population − *Old*.population
from   PopulationData **as** *Old* **cross join** PopulationData **as** *New*
where *Old*.countryCode = *New*.countryCode
        and *Old*.censusYear = 2014 **and** *New*.censusYear = 2015

Figure 5.20   Relational schema and query based on ORM schema (a) in Figure 5.19

Figure 5.20 shows the relational schema mapped from ORM schema (a) in Figure 5.19, together with the SQL code for a query to derive the population change for each country. For each country, the derivation needs to access two different rows from the same table, so a self-join is used.

Figure 5.20 shows the relational schema mapped from ORM schema (b) in Figure 5.19, together with the SQL code for the population change. For each country, both population figures are on the same row, so the derivation is much simpler.

Country (<u>countryCode,</u> populationIn2014, populationIn2015)

SQL code for query to derive the population change:

select countryCode, populationIn2015 − populationIn2014
from   Country

Figure 5.21   Relational schema and query based on ORM schema (b) in Figure 5.19

The next two steps (4 and 5) of the schema optimization procedure transform a set of mutually exclusive roles (see Figure 5.22).

Step 4 transforms a set of n exclusive unaries ($n \geq 2$) to a single binary, thus reducing n columns in the relational table for the object type to one. The larger the value of n, the more worthwhile it is to perform the transform. The former exclusion constraint is now simply enforced by the primary key constraint, and the new value constraint is easily enforced by a check clause.

Figure 5.1 considered earlier provided a simple example of optimization step 4, where Person is male and Person is female predicates may be replaced by the binary fact type Person has Gender {'M', 'F'}.

Step 5 transforms a set of n binaries ($n \geq 2$) to two binaries, by applying predicate generalization. The source set of binary fact types are functional, with an exclusion constraint over the roles with a simple uniqueness constraint. The target schema extracts an object type that is value-constrained to n items, one for each of the original binaries. The larger the value of n, the more worthwhile it is to perform this transform.

4

Generalize each set of *n* mutually exclusive unaries ($n \geq 2$) to a functional binary by extracting an object type with *n* values.

5
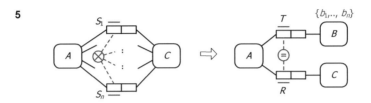

If *A* hosts *n* exclusive, functional roles ($n \geq 2$) in 1:*m* predicates with *C*,
   and *C* has no other functional role
then replace these *n* predicates by two binaries, by extracting *B* $\{b_1,.., b_n\}$ as shown.

Figure 5.22   Optimization steps 4 and 5: further aspects of mutually exclusive roles

To illustrate optimization step 5, consider the ORM schema and its relational map shown in Figure 5.23. Here each bank transaction involves exactly one of the following: a deposit by the user; a withdrawal by the user; interest applied by the bank; a fee charged by the bank. As an optional exercise, transform this using step 5 before reading on.

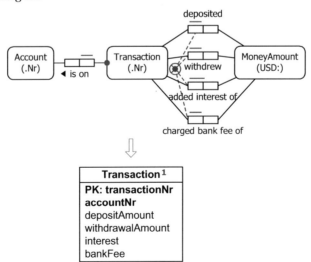

[1] **exactly one of** depositAmount, withdrawalAmount, interest, bankFee **is not null**.

Figure 5.23   An ORM schema and its relational map before optimization

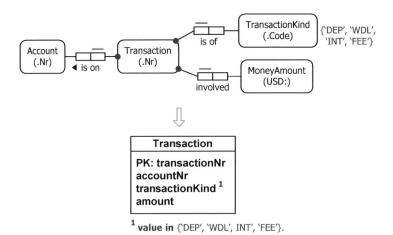

Figure 5.24   The schemas obtained after optimizing the schemas in Figure 5.23

Figure 5.24 shows the optimized ORM schema and its relational map after apply-ing optimization step 5. Further examples of the conceptual schema optimization procedure discussed so far are provided in chapter 14 of Halpin & Morgan (2008).

The final step (step 6) of the optimization procedure is to apply any relevant role reduction (role elimination and role redirection) transforms (see Figure 5.25). For examples of these transforms, see the discussion at the end of the previous section (Section 5.1).

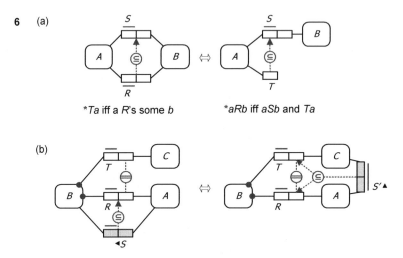

Where applicable, apply role elimination transforms (e.g. pattern (a) above) or role redirection transforms (e.g. pattern (b) above).

Figure 5.25   Optimization step 6: Apply role reduction transforms

Exercise 5.2

1.

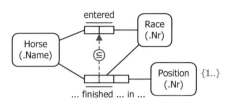

   (a) The above ORM schema maps to how many tables?

   (b) Optimize the above ORM schema.

   (c) Your optimized ORM schema maps to how many tables?

2. Consider the following ORM schema.

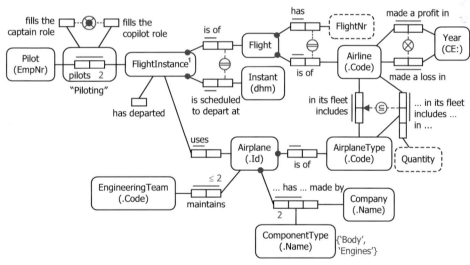

[1] **Each** FlightInstance has **at most one** Piloting **that** fills the captain role
       and has **at most one** Piloting **that** fills the copilot role.

   (a) This ORM schema Rmaps to how many tables?

   (b) Optimize the ORM schema.

   (c) Your optimized ORM schema maps to how many tables?

   (d) Rmap your solution to (b). Annotate the schema to include all constraints.
       Use either the horizontal relational notation, or the vertical notation used by
       NORMA.

5.3   Database Reengineering

ORM is useful not only for designing a new database, but also for redesigning or modifying an existing database that needs improvement. In practice, some existing databases need modification because they are inaccurate, incomplete, inefficient, or unclear (or any combination of the above). If the database is already populated with data, the *reengineering* process consists of four stages, as summarized in Figure 5.26. In this book, we assume the database is implemented in a relational DBMS.

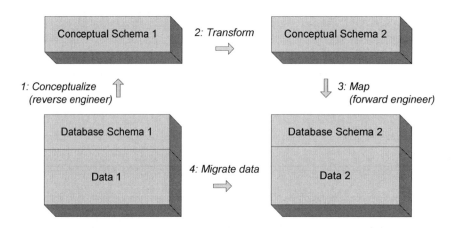

Figure 5.26   The four stages in reengineering a database

In stage 1, we *conceptualize* the relational database by *reverse engineering* its relational schema to an ORM schema. In stage 2, we *transform* the conceptual schema to ensure that it captures any required semantics lost in the original relational schema, and perform any relevant conceptual schema optimization transforms as discussed in the previous section. In stage 3, we use the Rmap procedure to *map* (or *forward engineer*) the new ORM schema to a new relational schema. If the original database was populated with data, stage 4 involves *migrating the data* from the old database to the new database.

In principle, much of the database reengineering process could be automated, but human input is typically needed to ensure that the final result is semantically correct and easy to understand.

The next section includes a lengthy exercise that covers the four stages of the reengineering process. To complete this exercise yourself, you need some background in normalization and SQL. These topics are discussed in depth in Halpin & Morgan (2008), as well as many other books. If you lack the relevant background, you should still gain some benefit by looking over the exercise and then checking the solution provided in the Answers section at the back of this book.

5.4   Solar System Exercise

Part 1

The SQL Server diagram shown below depicts the main aspects of a relational database schema used to record details about the planets and dwarf planets[5] in our solar system. The application developers do not fully understand the schema, and suspect that some aspects of the schema may be incomplete or even unsafe. Also, the database has performance problems mainly because of the number of table joins required for common queries. The tables were originally thrown together with little design discipline by someone who has now left the application team.

The following table lists all the attributes of the various tables, along with their data types.

Attribute	Data type
author	**nvarchar**(30)
bodyName	**nvarchar**(15)
bookTitle	**nvarchar**(30)
discoverer	**nvarchar**(30)
foreignLanguage	**nvarchar**(15)
foreignName	**nvarchar**(15)
gasFormula	**nvarchar**(5)

---

[5] http://en.wikipedia.org/wiki/Dwarf_planets

gasName	nvarchar(20)
isInnerDwarfPlanet	bit
isPlanet	bit
isPlutoid	bit
nameOrigin	nvarchar(40)
percentage	decimal(5,3)
property	nvarchar(15)
yearDiscovered	smallint
yearPublished	smallint

Because of your expertise in conceptual modeling, you are hired to provide a conceptual model of the application domain, so that a clear and complete picture of the universe of discourse is available. Moreover, you are asked to provide a new relational design that is both normalized and efficient, if this is possible.

In practice, such a reengineering task usually requires dialog with the domain expert(s) to clarify aspects of the UoD, including identification of missing constraints. For this exercise, I have provided explanations for much of the data, but you will still have to use your own common sense to complete the picture.

If you have access to Microsoft SQL Server, you can perform the exercise directly in SQL Server by first downloading the original SQL Server 2008 database (Solar-Body1). The database includes sample data, and is available for you to download as the file SolarBody1.zip from the following URL: http://1drv.ms/1QjBXrD. If you use a different DBMS, you can try to import the schema and sample data into your own system. From this point onwards, SQL Server is assumed.

Although the relational schema includes primary key declarations, it is missing all foreign key constraints as well as several other constraints that need to be enforced. Moreover, it includes some non-implied functional dependencies due to uncontrolled denormalization. Some of the missing constraints are "obvious", and some others may be inferred from the brief, incomplete description that follows.

In addition, rows of data are provided for each table so you can apply ORM CSDP Step 1. Though useful, the sample data are not fully significant (i.e. not all constraints may be deduced from them).

In this UoD, a solar body is either a planet or dwarf planet. An inner dwarf planet is a dwarf planet that lies inside the orbit of Neptune. A plutoid is a dwarf planet that lies outside the orbit of Neptune (see https://en.wikipedia.org/wiki/Plutoid). The discoverer of Haumea is disputed, and a special string value "???" is used to indicate this (*Note*: "???" is an actual value, not a null).

Although solar bodies are identified by their English name, their names in Malay and Greek may also be recorded (no other foreign languages are of interest). If a solar body has an atmosphere its main gases may be recorded, as well as the percentage composition. If an atmospheric gas is odorless or flammable, this is recorded (no other gas properties are of interest).

If a book by a single author has been written about one or more planets, this may be recorded, as well as the sole author and whether the book is fiction or non-fiction.

The current population of the database is shown below, with the primary key of each table underlined.

SolarBody:

bodyName	nameOrigin	isPlanet	isPlutoid	isInnerDwarfPlanet
Ceres	Roman goddess of the harvest	0	0	1
Earth	NULL	1	0	0
Eris	Greek goddess of discord	0	1	0
Haumea	Hawaiian goddess of fertility	0	1	0
Jupiter	Roman king of the gods	1	0	0
Makemake	Rapanui creator of humanity	0	1	0
Mars	Roman god of war	1	0	0
Mercury	Roman messenger god	1	0	0
Neptune	Roman god of the sea	1	0	0
Pluto	Roman god of the underworld	0	1	0
Saturn	Roman god of agriculture	1	0	0
Uranus	Roman sky god	1	0	0
Venus	Roman god of love	1	0	0

Discovery:

bodyName	discoverer	yearDiscovered
Ceres	Guiseppe Piazzi	1801
Eris	Chad Trujillo	2005
Eris	David Rabinowitz	2005
Eris	Michael Brown	2005
Haumea	???	2003
Makemake	Chad Trujillo	2005
Makemake	David Rabinowitz	2005
Makemake	Micheal Brown	2005
Neptune	Johan Gottfried Galle	1846
Neptune	John Couch Adams	1846
Neptune	Urbain Le Verrier	1846
Pluto	Clyde Tombaugh	1930
Uranus	William Herschel	1781

ForeignNames:

bodyName	foreignLanguage	foreignName
Earth	Greek	Gaea
Earth	Malay	Bumi
Jupiter	Greek	Zeus
Jupiter	Malay	Musytari
Mars	Greek	Ares
Mars	Malay	Marikh
Mercury	Greek	Hermes
Mercury	Malay	Utarid
Neptune	Greek	Poseidon
Neptune	Malay	Neptun
Pluto	Greek	Pluto
Pluto	Malay	Pluto
Saturn	Greek	Kronos
Saturn	Malay	Zuhal
Uranus	Greek	Uranos
Uranus	Malay	Uranus
Venus	Greek	Aphrodite
Venus	Malay	Zuhrah

Atmosphere:

bodyName	gasFormula	gasName
Earth	Ar	argon
Earth	CO2	carbon dioxide
Earth	N2	nitrogen
Earth	O2	oxygen
Jupiter	CH4	methane
Jupiter	H2	hydrogen
Jupiter	He	helium
Mars	Ar	argon
Mars	CO	carbon monoxide
Mars	CO2	carbon dioxide
Mars	N2	nitrogen
Mars	O2	oxygen
Mercury	CO	carbon monoxide
Mercury	H2	hydrogen
Mercury	He	helium
Mercury	O2	oxygen
Neptune	CH4	methane
Neptune	H2	hydrogen
Neptune	He	helium
Pluto	N2	nitrogen
Saturn	CH4	methane
Saturn	H2	hydrogen
Saturn	He	helium
Uranus	CH4	methane
Uranus	H2	hydrogen
Uranus	He	helium
Venus	CO2	carbon dioxide
Venus	N2	nitrogen
Venus	SO2	sulfur dioxide

AtmospherePercent:

bodyName	gasFormula	percentage
Earth	Ar	0.930
Earth	CO2	0.040
Earth	N2	78.000
Earth	O2	21.000
Jupiter	CH4	0.300
Jupiter	H2	89.800
Jupiter	He	10.200
Mars	Ar	1.600
Mars	CO	0.080
Mars	CO2	95.300
Mars	N2	2.700
Mars	O2	0.130
Mercury	CO	0.080
Mercury	H2	22.000
Mercury	He	6.000
Mercury	O2	42.000
Neptune	CH4	1.500
Neptune	H2	80.000
Neptune	He	18.000
Pluto	N2	90.000
Saturn	CH4	0.400
Saturn	H2	96.000
Saturn	He	3.000
Uranus	CH4	2.300
Uranus	H2	83.000
Uranus	He	15.000
Venus	CO2	96.500
Venus	N2	3.500
Venus	SO2	0.015

GasProperty:

gasFormula	property
Ar	odorless
CH4	flammable
CH4	odorless
CO	flammable
CO	odorless
CO2	odorless
H2	flammable
H2	odorless
He	odorless
N2	odorless
O2	odorless

Book:

bookTitle	author	yearPublished
A Princess of Mars	Edgar Rice Burroughs	1917
Jupiter: A Novel (Grand Tour)	Ben Bova	2002
Mars: a Cosmic Stepping Stone	Kevin Nolan	2007
Melbourne and Mars	Joseph Frazer	1889
Mission to Mars	Michael Collins	1990
The Gods of Mars	Edgar Rice Burroughs	1918
The War of the Worlds	H. G. Wells	1898

FictionBookTopic:

bodyName	bookTitle
Earth	Melbourne and Mars
Earth	The War of the Worlds
Jupiter	Jupiter: A Novel (Grand Tour)
Mars	A Princess of Mars
Mars	Melbourne and Mars
Mars	The Gods of Mars
Mars	The War of the Worlds

NonFictionBookTopic:

bodyName	bookTitle
Earth	Mission to Mars
Mars	Mars: a Cosmic Stepping Stone
Mars	Mission to Mars

1. Which table schemes in the original schema are not fully normalized? Explain briefly what design flaws cause them to be denormalized.

As the first step towards re-engineering the application to remove any redundancy problems and improve its performance, carry out the following reverse-engineering task[6].

2. *Reverse-engineer* the relational schema to an ORM conceptual schema in NORMA. For this small schema, it is best to do this manually, using the sample data as input to the CSDP, and then entering the conceptual schema as an ORM schema in

---

[6] In Parts 2 and 3, you will complete the re-engineering process by optimizing the conceptual schema, mapping it to a more efficient relational schema, performing data migration from the old tables to populate it, and recoding the focused queries for the new design.

NORMA, and setting the data types to those listed earlier. Do *not* concern yourself with efficiency or optimization at this stage. Your ORM schema, while being redundancy free with all fact types atomic, should in other respects directly reflect the design decisions made in the original relational schema as to what are the facts of interest. *Include all constraints* (graphical or textual) that apply to the application domain, including those constraints omitted from the original relational schema.

Download the original database stored in the file SolarBody1.zip from http://1drv.ms/1QjBXrD. Unzip the file (right-click and choose Extract All) to create the folder SolarBody1 containing the data file SolarBody1.MDF and the log file SolarBody1_log.LDF.

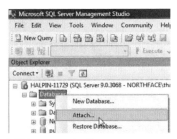

Now open SQL Server Management Studio and connect. To attach the database, right-click Databases, choose Attach..., press Add (see screenshot).

Now browse to the location of Solar-Body1.MDF, press OK, then press OK again.

To select the contents of the `SolarBody` table, choose NewQuery from the main menu, type "`select * from SolarBody`" and press F5 (or "! Execute") to execute the query.

3. Using this original database, specify and execute the following focused queries in SQL. These queries will help you appreciate how awkward the original design is for such tasks.

(a) For each solar body, list (on the same row) its body type (Planet, Plutoid, InnerDwarfPlanet), and year discovered (if known). The column headers and some sample rows from the query result are shown below:

```
bodyName      bodytype            yearDiscovered
-----------   -----------------   --------------
Ceres         InnerDwarfPlanet    1801
Eris          Plutoid             2005
Neptune       Planet              1846
Mars          Planet              NULL
```

(b) For each solar body, list (on the same row) its name, name origin, and Greek and Malay names (if recorded). The column headers and some sample rows from the query result are shown below:

```
bodyName      nameOrigin                     greekName   malayName
------------  -----------------------------  ----------  ------------
Ceres         Roman goddess of the harvest   NULL        NULL
Earth         NULL                           Gaea        Bumi
Jupiter       Roman king of the gods         Zeus        Musytari
```

(c) For each planet, list (on the same row) its name, as well as the title, author, and book type (fiction, nonfiction) of each book about it (if any). The column headers and some sample rows from the query result are shown below:

```
bodyName        bookTitle             author             bookType
------------    ------------------    -----------------  -----------
Earth           Melbourne and Mars    Joseph Frazer      fiction
Earth           Mission to Mars       Michael Collins    nonfiction
Mars            Melbourne and Mars    Joseph Frazer      fiction
Venus           NULL                  NULL               NULL
```

Solar System Exercise

Part 2

The business domain is the same as for Part 1. The ORM schema reverse engineered from the original SolarBody1 database is displayed in the Answers section at the back of this book, and is available as the NORMA file SolarBody1.orm at the following URL: http://1drv.ms/1WVF4VC.

Download this file as input for the following tasks to complete the modification, optimization, and relational mapping phase of the reengineering procedure

1. *Transform* the ORM schema to an *"optimized conceptual schema"* that minimizes the number of tables obtained if the Rmap procedure is applied, and optimizes the design efficiency of individual tables.

2. If using a model for which the relational view extension is not active, right-click anywhere on the document window, select Extension Manager from the context menu, check Relational View, then press OK. The relational view extension is now enabled.

   Forward-engineer your optimized conceptual schema to a relational database diagram displayed on the Relational View page. Do not display the data types. Ensure all tables and columns are named well (add fact type names, role names and abbreviations if needed to ensure this).

   Rearrange the relational diagram to improve layout, and reorder columns within tables to your preferred order.

   Annotate the relational schema diagram to *display all constraints*, using footnote numbers and footnote text where needed.

Solar System Exercise
Part 3

The original relational schema for the denormalized SolarBody1 database is repeated below, and the final relational schema obtained by conceptual optimization and mapping in Part 2 is displayed below it.

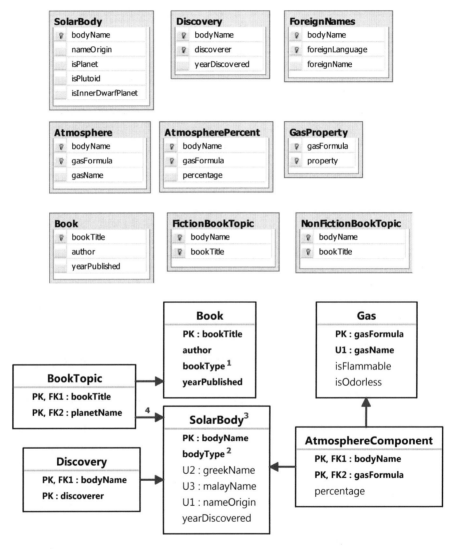

[1] **value in** {'fiction', 'nonfiction'}.

[2] **value in** {'Planet', 'InnerDwarfPlanet', 'Plutoid'}.

[3] greekName **is not null iff** malayName **is not null**.

[4] **only where** SolarBody.bodyType = 'Planet'.

The SQL Server DDL to create this SolarBody2DB schema is available as the text file SolarBody2DB.sql at the following URL: http://1drv.ms/1lmHS2e. Download this file as input for the following tasks to complete the data migration and query rewriting phase of the reengineering procedure. If using a DBMS other than SQL Server, make any minor changes needed to the script to have it create the database in your system. The following instructions assume you are using SQL Server.

Run SQL Server Management Studio, choose New Query to open a query window, open the SolarBody2DB.sql file and execute this DDL code (press F5 or the Execute button): you may need to select and run just the code to create the database first, then select and run the other code later. Now right click the SolarBody2DB database folder in Object Explorer, and choose Refresh from the context menu. Now expand the Tables folder for this database. The SolarBody2DB tables should now appear in the tables list.

1. Write SQL code to perform the *data migration* needed to populate the Solar-Body2DB database. You can do this within SolarBody2DB by starting with the clause **use** SolarBody1, and then qualifying the target tables with the prefix Solar-Body2DB.dbo. If one table has a foreign key that references another table, populate the target (referenced) table before you populate the source (referencing) table. For the BookTopic table, ensure that the rows are ordered by the book title.

    Hints: First try a query on the SolarBody1 database that returns the expected rows for the new table as the result; then convert it into an insert-into statement, ensuring that the result columns match the column order in the target table (expand the target table to see its column order). If your query has multiple joins, specify one join at a time with the join conditions, before introducing the next join.

2. Using your populated SolarBody2DB database, specify and execute the three queries from Part 1 in SQL (reproduced below).

    Note: If you are unable to provide the data migration code for a table used in one of the following queries, then populate the table manually using the sample data.

    (a) For each solar body, list (on the same row) its body type (Planet, Plutoid, In-nerDwarfPlanet), and year discovered (if known).

    (b) For each solar body, list (on the same row) its name, name origin, and Greek and Malay names (if recorded).

    (c) For each planet, list (on the same row) its name, as well as the title, author, and book type (fiction, nonfiction) of each book about it (if any).

6 Some Data Model Patterns

This chapter discusses some data modeling patterns for dealing with temporal aspects of information systems (e.g. maintaining history of fact type populations and recording history of role subtype migration), as well as different kinds of collection structures (sets, ordered sets, bags, multisets, and sequences).

6.1   Temporal Aspects

Many data models involve object types that are temporal in nature. We distinguish between *Instant* (a point in time, e.g. 2015 November 14, 10:28 a.m. UTC), *Duration* (a length of time, e.g. 5 days) and *Period* (an anchored duration in time, e.g. 2015 November 15 .. 2015 November 20). The precision with which we record a temporal value is known as *temporal granularity*. For example, Date is an appropriate object type for recording when an event occurred if the temporal granularity is one day.

For typical business domains, the population of most of the relevant fact types varies over time. If we are interested only in the current (*valid time*) or most recently recorded (*transaction time*) population, *snapshot fact types* are sufficient (e.g. Patient has Temperature). If instead we wish to maintain *history* of a snapshot fact type's population, we need to introduce a temporal object type of the desired granularity.

How we do this depends on whether the original fact type is functional (all but one role is spanned by a simple uniqueness constraint) or not. Figure 6.1 shows four ways to model *history* for the *functional fact type* Patient has Temperature.

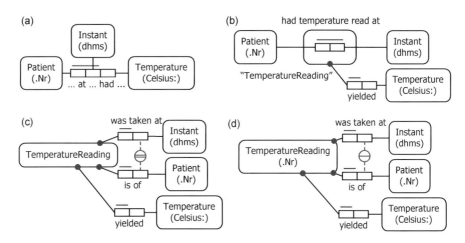

Figure 6.1   Four ways to maintain history for a functional fact type

Figure 6.1(a) uses a flattened fact type that introduces Instant (with a granularity of one second) into the key of the original snapshot fact type. Depending on the example, a different temporal object type could be used instead of Instant (e.g. Date or Period). Figure 6.1(b) and Figure 6.1(c) use equivalent nested or coreferenced approaches, while Figure 6.1(d) introduces a simple identification scheme for the entity type TemperatureReading.

The four modeling solutions illustrated in Figure 6.1 may be straightforwardly adapted to model history for any functional fact type, and thus provide modeling patterns for this kind of situation.

An *event* is either a *point event*, occurring at a single time (e.g. a person's birth) or a *period event*, occurring over a non-zero period of time (e.g. a conference). If the snapshot fact type is *non-functional* (e.g. many-to-many) and concerns a *once-only* (non-repeatable) *event*, temporal details for it may be recorded in separate fact types. For example, the schema in Figure 6.2 shows one way to model temporal details for the fact type Person toured Country only once. In this case, instances of OnceOnlyTour are period events for which we record the start date and optionally an end date. You could also model once-only tours using coreference or a simple identifier.

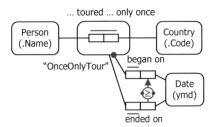

Figure 6.2   One way to model temporal details for once-only period events.

If the snapshot fact type is both *non-functional and repeatable* (it records a repeatable event) then there are various ways to model temporal details for it. For example, the many-to-many fact type Person visited Country is repeatable, because it is possible for the same person to visit the same country more than once. Since a tour is a period event, we can objectify the fact type Person began a tour of Country on Date, and then attach the optional end date fact type, as shown in Figure 6.3.

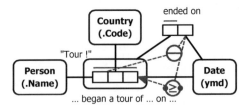

Figure 6.3   One way to model temporal details for repeatable period events.

The external uniqueness constraint in Figure 6.3 ensures that each person, country and tour end date has only one tour start date. NORMA verbalizes this constraint as follows:

> **For each** Person, Country, **and** Date₁,
> **there is at most one** Tour **such that**
> **that** Person began a tour of **that** Country on **some** Date
> **where that** Country is involved in **that** Tour **that** ended on **that** Date₁.

The value-comparison constraint in Figure 6.3 ensures that a tour cannot end before it starts. NORMA treats this as a constraint between the end-date role and the role hosted by Date in the implied fact type between Tour and Date that results from the objectification. By default, NORMA assigns the readings "Tour involves / is involved in Date" to this implied fact type. To improve the readings, select and edit the implied fact type reading in the ORM Model Browser, then the inverse reading using the ORM reading Editor to "Tour started on Date" as shown below.

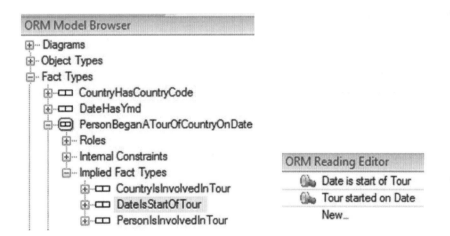

NORMA now verbalizes the value-comparison constraint as follows:

> **For each** Tour,
> **if that** Tour ended on **some** Date₁
> **and** started on **some** Date₂
> **then** Date₁ **is greater than or equal to** Date₂.

Figure 6.4 shows three other ways in which to model temporal details for period events. Figure 6.4(a) uses coreferencing instead of nesting, and Figure 6.4(b) introduces a simple, visible identifier (TourId) to identify tours. With this approach, Tour is no longer independent, and there are now two non-preferred external uniqueness constraints.

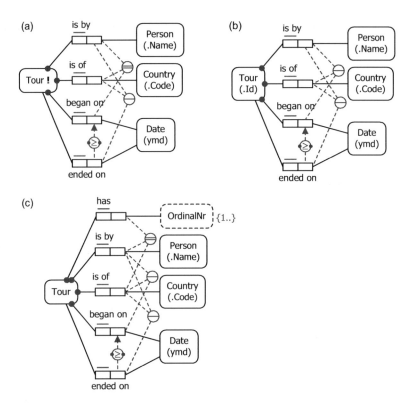

Figure 6.4   Three other ways to model temporal details for repeatable period events.

Figure 6.4(c) introduces an ordinal number as part of the identification scheme for Tour. For example, the first tour by a person to a given country has the ordinal number 1, and the second tour (if any) by that person to the same country has the ordinal number 2. The four modeling solutions in Figure 6.3 and Figure 6.4 may easily be adapted to fit other cases of this kind.

An object type in ORM is said to be a *rigid type* if and only if each of its instances must belong to that type for its whole lifetime (in the business domain being modeled). Examples of rigid types include Person and Car. In this book, we classify all object types that are not rigid as *role types*. Moreover, the only role types we consider are *subtypes*. Unlike some ontological frameworks, we use the term "role type" liberally to cover cases based on roles played by objects as well as phases or states of objects. Examples of role subtypes include Employee and Registered Car (assuming instances may leave that type and still remain in the UoD).

Migration between rigid types is impossible (e.g. a person cannot become a car) but for role subtypes of a common supertype (e.g. Person) an object may migrate from a *temporary role type* (e.g. Child) to another temporary role type (e.g. Teenager) or to a *permanent role type* (e.g. Adult).

The ORM schema in Figure 6.5 includes Child, Teenager and Adult as role sub-types of Person. In this UoD, we use these subtype names for subtypes that are mutually exclusive but not collectively exhaustive (e.g. we might consider PreTeenager as a state between Child and Teenager for which no specific facts are of interest).

Figure 6.5 depicts me as an instance of these subtypes, using a dot inside the ORM subtype shapes as well as photos of myself at these three stages of my lifetime. The state transition graph at the bottom of Figure 6.5 indicates that over time a person may change its state from child to teenager to adult, in that order. Since reincarnation is not modeled in this UoD, no loops are allowed in the transition graph (e.g. an adult cannot later become a child). So this is a case of *linear state transitions*.

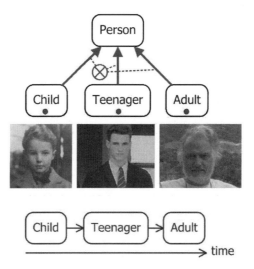

Figure 6.5   **Migration between role subtypes based on linear state transitions.**

Suppose that, as part of a longitudinal study, specific details are recorded about people at the time they play roles that are related via linear state transitions. For example, only when a person is a child is his or her favorite fairy tale recorded, only when a person is a teenager is his or her favorite comic recorded, and only when a person is an adult is his or her favorite book recorded. Figure 6.6 shows one way to model this situation. For simplicity, rigid reference schemes are assumed.

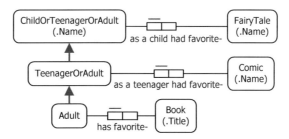

Figure 6.6   **One way to maintaining history as a person changes roles**

The approach adopted in Figure 6.6 is called the *successive disjunctions pattern*, since each supertype may be named using the logical disjunction operator "or" to cover more objects than its direct subtype. If Child, Teenager and Adult were collectively exhaustive subtypes of Person, the top supertype could be named "Person".

An alternative and more flexible approach to model the situation is to use the *once-only role playing pattern*, as shown in Figure 6.7. Here the specific details are attached to subtypes corresponding to the playing of the relevant roles. The footnoted constraint is a dynamic constraint on the state transitions. LifeRolePlaying could also be modeled by coreferencing rather than nesting.

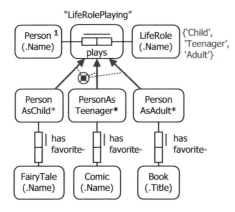

* **Each** PersonAsChild **is defined as a** LifeRolePlaying **that** involves LifeRole 'Child'.
* **Each** PersonAsTeenager **is defined as a** LifeRolePlaying **that** involves LifeRole 'Teenager'.
* **Each** PersonAsAdult **is defined as a** LifeRolePlaying **that** involves LifeRole 'Adult'.

[1] **For each** Person,
  in case previous lifeRole =
      'Child':   **added** lifeRole = 'Teenager'
      'Teenager': **added** lifeRole = 'Adult'
  end cases.

Figure 6.7   Another way to maintain history as a person changes roles

Some kinds of role playing may be *repeated*, allowing loops in the role state transition graph, as shown in Figure 6.8. For example, a person playing the married role may later play a widowed or divorced role, and later again play the married role. As another example, a person may play a manager role more than once.

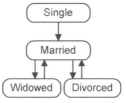

Figure 6.8   A non-linear state-transition graph, allowing loops

To handle such cases, we simply superimpose one of our patterns for history of changeable fact types onto the once-only role playing pattern. For example, ignoring the dynamic constraint on state transitions, maintenance of history over nonlinear role migration for our marriage example may be modeled as shown in Figure 6.9.

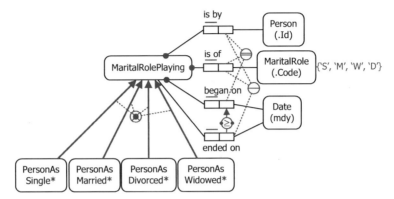

*__Each__ PersonAsSingle __is defined as a__ MaritalRolePlaying __that__ is of MaritalRole 'S'.
*__Each__ PersonAsMarried __is defined as a__ MaritalRolePlaying __that__ is of MaritalRole 'M'.
*__Each__ PersonAsDivorced __is defined as a__ MaritalRolePlaying __that__ is of MaritalRole 'D'.
*__Each__ PersonAsWidowed __is defined a__ MaritalRolePlaying __that__ is of MaritalRole 'W'.

Figure 6.9   One way of modeling history of non-linear role migration

Figure 6.10(a) shows a general repeatable role playing pattern based on this approach. This assumes that an actor may begin or end a given role at most once on the same date. If this is not true, replace Date by a finer temporal object type to ensure the uniqueness, e.g. Instant.

The pattern in Figure 6.10(a) also allows that an actor may begin or end multiple roles on the same date. If this is not true, use the simpler external uniqueness constraint pattern shown in Figure 6.10(b).

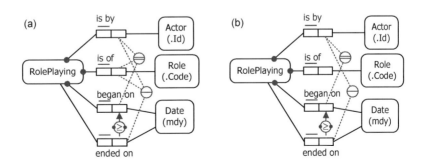

Figure 6.10   A general pattern for modeling history of repeatable role playing

Other options for repeatable role playing patterns are obtained by adapting the other solutions for repeatable fact types discussed earlier. For example, introduce a simple identifier for RolePlaying, or include an ordinal number as part of its identification.

For further discussion of temporal modeling issues in ORM, see section 14.3 of Halpin & Morgan (2008).

Exercise 6.1

---

1. Explain briefly what's wrong with the following ORM schema. Assume that reference schemes are supplied.

2. A jūdōka (judo player) is either a novice (kyū grade) or a black belt holder (dan grade). The following ORM schema is intended to record a player's favorite technique (waza) when they were a novice, and their favorite technique and favorite form (kata) when they are a dan grade. A dan grade's favorite technique need not be the same as his/her favorite technique when he/she was a kyū grade. The following model is intended to record full history, but fails to do so.

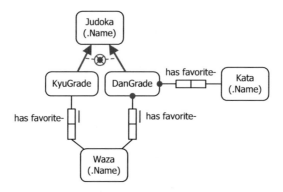

   Provide an alternative ORM schema that does allow such history to be recorded.

3. A given project team has 3 team roles: Captain (C), Vice-Captain (VC), Ordinary Member (OM). The project lasts for a long time. On any given date, a student has at most one of these roles. Over time, a student may play the same role many

times (e.g. move from VC to C and then back to VC). The following model is intended to record full history, but fails to do so. Modify and/or add external uniqueness constraints to provide an alternative ORM schema that does allow such history to be recorded.

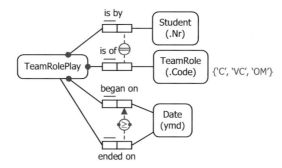

4. The following ORM schema is used to record which exam questions students have currently completed.

Modify the schema to enable a history to be kept of when students complete questions. Use a temporal granularity of 1 second, and assume that a student cannot complete more than one question at any given time.

5. At a given university, academics may be a teacher or researcher, but not both at the same time. The same employee may move between these two positions many times.

When working as a teacher, a score is kept of how well he/she teaches. When working as a researcher, a rank is determined for his/her research output. Sample data are shown below for one employee.

Specify an ORM schema to enable full history of such details to be maintained.

Employee	Position	Start	End	Teaching Score	Research Rank
101	Teacher	2007-01-01	2007-12-31	5	–
101	Researcher	2008-01-01	2014-12-31	–	B+
101	Teacher	2015-01-01	–	6	–

6.2   Collection Types

This section discusses ways of modeling the following kinds of collections in ORM: sets; ordered sets; bags; and sequences.

In mathematics, a *set* is an unordered collection of items, where duplication has no significance. For example, the set {a, b} is identical to the set {b, a} as well as to the set {a, a, b}. In information systems modeling, a set is defined somewhat differently as an *unordered collection with no duplicates*, so {a, a, b} would not be a set in this sense, since item *a* is duplicated.

In ORM, the populations of all fact types are sets of facts. If ever we wish to model a set of objects, we simply use *named* sets. Figure 6.11 provides a simple example. Although some modeling approaches support direct modeling of unnamed sets, in practice this usually leads to unneeded complexity. For some discussion on this issue, see section 10.4 of Halpin & Morgan (2008).

Figure 6.11   Modeling soccer teams as sets of soccer players

In information modeling, an *ordered set* is an *ordered collection of items with no duplicates*. For example, if a book has known authors, these authors are listed in a certain order (e.g. with major authors listed earlier, or simply ordered by name). If we are not interested in this order, we can model authorship facts using the simple schema shown in Figure 6.12(a).

However, if the order of the authors is of interest, the ordered set of authors may be modeled by introducing a Position type to record each author's place in the author list, as shown in Figure 6.12(b). Although not depicted graphically, ideally we should also constrain the position values for a given book to be sequential from 1.

Note the pattern of uniqueness constraints in Figure 6.12(b). The uniqueness constraint over the book and author roles ensures that each author appears only once in the book's author list (no duplicates). The uniqueness constraint over the book and position roles ensures that at most one author appears at any given position in the book's author list.

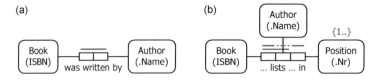

Figure 6.12   Treating author lists as (a) a set, and (b) an ordered set

As another example, consider the simplified relational metamodel fragment shown in Figure 6.13(a), where we confine ourselves to at most one relational schema, so a relational table can be identified by its name. A relational column may be identified by the combination of its name and its table. This schema treats a table simply as a set of columns.

In practice, the order of columns within a table is significant for layout purposes, so a table is then viewed as an ordered set of columns. Unlike the authorship example, where an author may write many books and vice versa, a column belongs to only one table. So to model the column order, the Position object type needs to be placed in a separate fact type, along with an external uniqueness constraint, as shown in Figure 6.13(b).

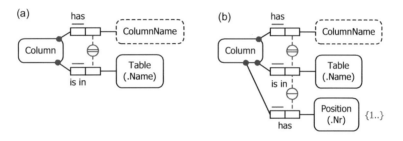

Figure 6.13   Treating tables as (a) a column set, and (b) an ordered column set

A *bag* (or *multiset*) is an *unordered collection that allows duplicates*. For example, the bag [a, b] is identical to the bag [b, a] but differs from the bag [a, a, b]. The ORM schema in Figure 6.14(a) allows recording what kinds of medals (gold, silver, or bronze) were awarded to countries. The extended ORM schema in Figure 6.14(b) uses a ternary fact type with Quantity to count how many medals of each kind were awarded to each country.

For example, in the summer Olympic games held so far, Costa Rica won one gold, one silver l and two bronze medals, so its bag of medal wards is [gold, silver, bronze, bronze]. This result would populate the ternary with the tuples ('CRC', 'gold', 1); ('CRC', 'silver', 1) and ('CRC', 'bronze' 2). For a full record of Olympic medal tallies, see https://en.wikipedia.org/wiki/All-time_Olympic_Games_medal_table.

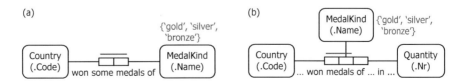

Figure 6.14   Modeling a country's medal awards as (a) a set and (b) a bag

A *sequence* is an *ordered bag* (i.e. *an ordered collection that allows duplicates*). For example, the sequences <*a, b*>, <*b, a*> and <*a, a, b*> are all different. As a trivial example, the ORM schema with some sample data in Figure 6.15(a) allows us to explicitly record which letters occur in which words. The extended schema in Figure 6.15(b) uses a ternary fact type with a Position object type inside the key to record at what position(s) the letters occur, thus modeling a word as a sequence of letters, not just a set of letters.

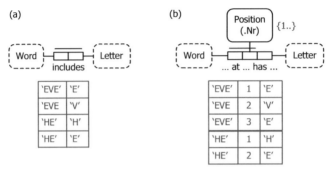

Figure 6.15   Modeling word letter contents as (a) a set and (b) a sequence

Exercise 6.2

_____

1. Which of the following statements is/are true?

      A   A multiset is also called an ordered set

      B   A sequence is an ordered bag

      C   Ordered sets allow duplicate entries

2. The following table is an extract from a report that records the places obtained by athletes in various races. No ties are allowed. Specify an ORM schema to allow recording of this information.

Race	Place	Athlete
1	1	John Smith
1	2	Bob Jones
...	...	...
2	1	John Smith
2	2	Fred Bloggs
...	...	...

3. The following simplified class diagram in the Unified Modeling Language (UML) depicts Employee as a class with attributes nr and name, and Country as a class with attributes code and name. For simplicity, attribute properties such as multiplicity, visibility and {id} markers are ignored, and the domain is restricted to a single UML schema.

   Specify a metamodel fragment in ORM to capture such class details, including the ordered position of each attribute in its class.

Employee	**Country**
nr name ...	code name ...

4. The following object-relation is used to store the sequence of teaching scores obtained by various academic employees at a university. Sample data for two employees are shown. Specify an ORM schema for this example.

Employee	*Teaching Scores*
101	5, 6, 6, 7
102	3, 3, 5

Appendix A: ORM Symbol Glossary

This ORM Symbol Glossary summarizes the main graphical symbols used in ORM.

Construct and Examples	Explanatory Comments
Entity type Country or Country or Country	Named soft rectangle, named hard rectangle, or named ellipse. The soft rectangle shape is the default.
Value type CountryCode or CountryCode or CountryCode	Named, dashed, soft rectangle (or hard rectangle or ellipse).
Entity type with popular reference mode Country (.code) Course (.code) Company (.name) Building (.nr)	Abbreviation for injective reference relationship to value type, e.g. Country — has / is of — CountryCode
Entity type with unit-based reference mode Height (cm:) Mass (kg:) Salary (USD:) Price (EUR:) Height (cm: Length) Salary (USD: Money) Price (EUR: Money)	Abbreviation for reference fact type, e.g. Height — has / is of — cmValue Optionally, the unit type may be displayed (as shown opposite).
Entity type with general reference mode Website (URL) Weblink (URL)	Abbreviation for reference fact types, e.g. Website — is identified by — URL Weblink — is identified by — URL
Independent object type Country ! CountryCode !	Instances of the type may exist, without playing any elementary fact roles.
External object type Address^	Object type is defined in another model. This notation is tentative (yet to be finalized).

Construct and Examples	Explanatory Comments
Predicate (unary, binary, ternary, etc.) 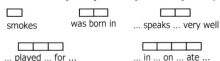	Ordered set of role boxes with at least one predicate reading in mixfix notation. If shown, object placeholders are denoted by "...". If placeholders are not shown, unaries are in prefix and binaries are in infix notation.
Duplicate type or predicate shape 	If an object type or predicate shape is displayed more than once (on the same page or different pages) it is shadowed.
Unary fact type 	Attaching a role box to an object type shape means that only instances of that object type may play that role (e.g. here, the smokes role may be played only by instances of the Person object type). A role name may be added in square brackets.
Binary fact type 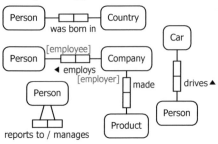	By default, predicate readings (binary or longer) are read left-to-right or top-to-bottom. An arrow-tip is used to display a different reading direction. Role names may be displayed in square brackets beside their role. Forward and inverse readings for binaries may be shown together, separated by "/".
Ternary fact type 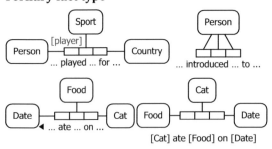	Role names may be added in square brackets. Arrow-tips are used to reverse the default left-right or top-down reading order. Reading orders other than forward and reverse are shown using named placeholders.

Construct and Examples	**Explanatory Comments**
Quaternary fact type 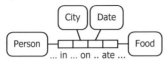	The comments for the ternary case apply here also. Fact types of higher arity (number of roles) are also permitted.
Objectification 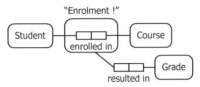	The enrolment fact type is objectified as an entity type whose instances can play roles. In this example, the objectification type is independent, so we can know about an enrolment before the grade is obtained.
Internal uniqueness constraint (UC) on unary 	These examples are equivalent. By default, fact types are assumed to be populated with sets of facts (not bags of facts), so no whole fact may be duplicated.
Internal UCs on a binary fact type 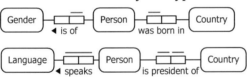	The examples show the 4 possible patterns: 1:n (one-to-many); n:1 (many-to-one); m:n (many-to-many); 1:1 (one-to-one).
Internal UCs on ternaries 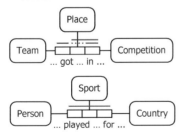	The first example has two, 2-role UCs: the top UC forbids ties; the other UC ensures that each team gets only place per competition (a dotted line excludes its role from the UC). The second example has a spanning UC (many-to-many-to-many). For an n-ary ($n > 2$) fact type to be atomic, each UC on it must span at least n–1 roles.

Construct and Examples	*Explanatory Comments*

Simple mandatory role constraint

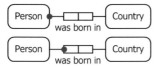

The example constraint means that each person was born in some country. The mandatory role dot may be placed at either end of the role connector.

Inclusive-or constraint

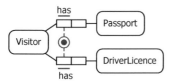

An inclusive-or constraint is also called a disjunctive mandatory role constraint. The constraint displays as a circled dot connected to the constrained roles. The example constraint means that each visitor noted in the model must have a passport or a driver licence (often spelt as "license" in the US) or both.

Preferred internal UC

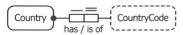

A double bar on a UC indicates it underlies the preferred reference scheme.

External UC

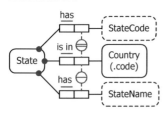

A double-bar indicates that the constrained roles provide the preferred reference for the object type at the other end. Here, each state is primarily identified by combining its country and state code. Each combination of country and state name also applies to only one state.

Object type value constraint

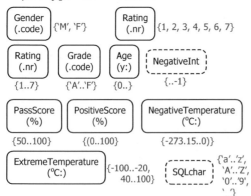

The allowed values may be specified as a list of discrete values and/or value ranges. The two examples shown opposite specify an enumerated list of values.
Ranges are inclusive of end values by default. Round brackets exclude an end value. Square brackets explicitly declare inclusion, e.g. the constraint on PositiveScore may also be specified as {(0..100]}. Multiple combinations may also be specified.

Construct and Examples	*Explanatory Comments*
Role value constraint 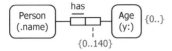	As for object type value constraints, but connected to the constrained role. Here, an age of a person must be at most 140 years.
Subset constraint 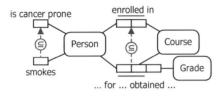	The arrow points from the subset end to the superset end (e.g. **if a** Person smokes **then that** Person is cancer prone). The role sequences at both ends must be compatible. A connection to the junction of 2 roles constrains that role pair.
Join subset constraint 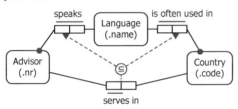	The constrained role pair at the superset end is projected from a role path that involves a conceptual join on Language. The constraint declares that if an advisor serves in a country then that advisor must speak a language that is often used in that country.
Exclusion constraint 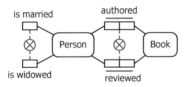	These exclusion constraints mean that no person is both married and widowed, and no person reviewed and authored the same book. Exclusion may apply between 2 or more compatible role sequences, possibly involving joins.
Exclusive-or constraint 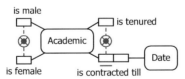	An exclusive-or constraint is simply the conjunction of an inclusive-or constraint and an exclusion constraint. Also known as an xor constraint.
Equality constraint 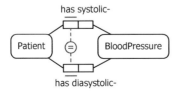	This equality constraint means that a patient's systolic BP is recorded if and only if his/her diastolic BP is recorded. An equality constraint may apply between 2 or more compatible role sequences, possibly involving joins.

Construct and Examples	Explanatory Comments

Derived fact type, and derivation rule

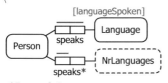

*For each** Person,
    nrLanguages = **count**(languageSpoken).

A fact type is either asserted, derived, or semiderived. A derived fact type is marked with an asterisk "*". A derivation rule is supplied. A double asterisk "**" indicates derived and stored (eager evaluation).

Semiderived fact type, and derivation rule

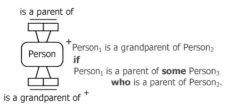

A fact type is semiderived if some of its instances may be derived, and some of its instances may be simply asserted. It is marked by "+" (half an asterisk). "++"indicates semiderived and stored (eager evaluation for derived instances).

Subtyping

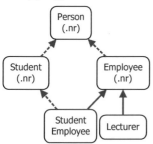

All subtypes are proper subtypes. An arrow runs from subtype to supertype. A solid arrow indicates a path to the subtype's preferred identifier (e.g. here, student employees are primarily identified by their employee number). A dashed arrow indicates the supertype has a different preferred identifier.

Subtyping constraints

A circled "X" indicates the subtypes are mutually exclusive. A circled dot indicates the supertype equals the union of the subtypes. The combination (xor constraint) indicates the subtypes partition the supertype (exclusive and exhaustive).

Construct and Examples	*Explanatory Comments*

Subtype derivation status

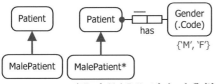

* **Each** MalePatient **is by definition some** Patient **who** has Gender 'M'.

is a parent of

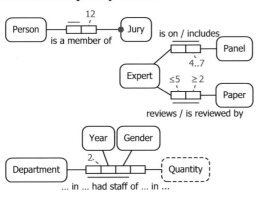

$^+$**Each derived** Grandparent **is by definition some** Person **who** is a parent of **some** Person **who** is a parent of **some** Person.

A subtype may be asserted, derived (denoted by "*"), or semiderived (denoted by "+"). If the subtype is asserted, it has no mark appended and has no derivation rule. If the subtype derived or semiderived, a derivation rule is supplied.

Internal frequency constraint

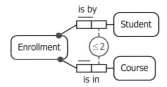

This constrains the number of times an occurring instance of a role or role sequence may appear in each population. Here: each jury has exactly 12 members; each panel that includes an expert includes at least 4 and at most 7 experts; each expert reviews at most 5 papers; each paper that is reviewed is reviewed by at least 2 experts; and each department and year that has staff numbers recorded in the quaternary appears there twice (once for each gender).

External frequency constraint

The example external frequency constraint has the following meaning. In this context, each combination of student and course relates to at most two enrolments (i.e. a student may enroll at most twice in the same course).

Construct and Examples	*Explanatory Comments*

Value-comparison constraint

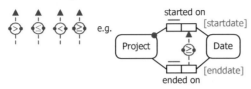

The example value-comparison constraint verbalizes as follows: **For each** Project, **if that** Project started on **some** Date$_1$ **and** ended on **some** Date$_2$ **then** Date$_2$ **is greater than or equal to** Date$_1$.

Object cardinality constraint

The example constraints ensure that at any given time there is at most one president and either 0 or at least 5 and at most 15 members of the UN Security Council.

Role cardinality constraint

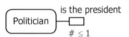

The example constraint ensures that at most one politician is the president (at any given time).

Ring constraints

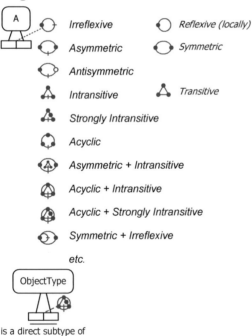

A ring predicate R is locally reflexive if and only if, for all x and y, xRy implies xRx. E.g. "knows" is locally but not globally reflexive. Reflexive, symmetric and transitive properties may also be enforced using semiderivation rather than by constraining asserted fact types.

The example constrains the subtyping relationship in ORM to be both acyclic (no cycles can be formed by a chain of subtyping connections) and strongly intransitive (no object type A can be both a direct subtype of another type B and an indirect subtype of B, where indirect subtyping means there is a chain of two or more subtyping relationships that lead from A to B).

Ring constraints may be combined only if they are compatible, and one is not implied by the other. ORM tools ensure that only legal combinations are allowed.

Construct and Examples	*Explanatory Comments*

Deontic constraints

Uniqueness   o—   ⊖

Mandatory   o   ◉

Subset, Equality, Exclusion   ⑤ ⑤ ⊗

Frequency   °f

Irreflexive	◖∶◗	Acyclic	
Asymmetric		Asym-Intrans	
Intransitive		Acyclic-Intrans	
Antisymmetric		Symmetric	
Strongly Intransitive		etc.	

E.g.

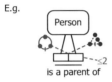

is a parent of

Unlike alethic constraints, deontic constraint shapes are colored blue rather than violet. Most include "o" for "obligatory". Deontic ring constraints instead use dashed lines.

In the parenthood example, the alethic frequency constraint ensures that each person has at most two parents, the alethic ring constraint ensures that parenthood is acyclic, and the deontic ring constraint makes it obligatory for parenthood to be strongly intransitive.

Textual constraints

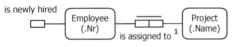

[1] **Each** Employee **who** is newly hired
   is assigned to **at most one** Project.

First-order constraints with no graphic notation may be expressed textually in the FORML 2 language. This example uses footnoting to capture a restricted uniqueness constraint.

Objectification display options

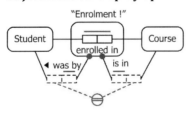

⊂⊃ Enrolment !

Internally, link fact types connect objectified associations to their component object types. By default, display of link fact types is suppressed. If displayed, link predicate shapes use dashed lines. Objectification types may also be displayed without their defining components, using an object type shape containing a small predicate shape, as in this Enrolment example.

Appendix B: Further Resources

Some Relevant References:

This book is a sequel to my previous book (listed below), which covers the fundamental concepts in ORM, as well as detailed instructions on how to use the main features of the NORMA tool.

> Halpin, T. 2015, *Object-Role Modeling Fundamentals*, Technics Publications.

The following book provides an in-depth coverage of ORM including a more formal treatment of its underlying theory. It includes hundreds of exercise questions with answers provided online for all odd-numbered questions. It also discusses other information modeling approaches such as ER, and UML, and how they relate to ORM. It provides a solid introduction to relational database theory and SQL, and both forward and reverse engineering between ORM and SQL. It also briefly discusses other database-related topics such as deductive databases and the semantic web.

> Halpin, T. & Morgan T. 2008, *Information Modeling and Relational Databases, 2nd edition*, Morgan Kaufmann.

The following paper discusses ORM reduction transformations that are not covered in the previous reference.

> Halpin, T., Carver, A. & Owen, K. 2007, 'Reduction Transformations in ORM', *On the Move to Meaningful Internet Systems 2007: OTM 2007 Workshops*, eds. R. Meersman, Z. Tari, P. Herrero et al., Vilamoura, Springer LNCS 4805, pp. 699-708.

The following journal articles provide brief overviews of ORM.

> Halpin, T. 2010, 'Object-Role Modeling: Principles and Benefits', *International Journal of Information Systems Modeling and Design*, Vol. 1, No. 1, IGI Global, pp. 32-54.
> Halpin, T. 2011, 'Fact-Orientation and Conceptual Logic', *Proc. 15th International EDOC Conference*, IEEE Computer Society, Helsinki, pp. 14-19.

Some Relevant Websites:

My website www.orm.net includes recent news about ORM as well as many other articles on ORM and related topics, and links to other relevant websites. The Resources page of this website also contains links to my articles that have been published in the online *Business Rules Journal* (http://www.brcommunity.com/). These include articles on ORM verbalization of business rules, modeling temporal aspects of information systems, data modeling for the semantic web using languages such as the Web Ontology Language (OWL), and logical data modeling for deductive databases using LogiQL.

The ORM Foundation website www.ORMFoundation.org includes a library with many ORM resources, including the Visio ORM2 stencil, as well an online forum for discussing ORM-related topics.

The Fact-Based Modeling Working Group (www.factbasedmodeling.org) is working on an exchange metamodel for fact-based modeling approaches such as ORM, with an aim to have it officially adopted by an industry or standards group.

The NORMA tool is available as a free plug-in to Microsoft Visual Studio (2005 or later edition). A Community Edition of Visual Studio 2015 is accessible at http://www.visualstudio.com/products/visual-studio-community-vs. The text on the license agreement for this edition includes the following conditions:

> "Here's how Visual Studio Community can be used in organizations:
> - An unlimited number of users within an organization can use Visual Studio Community for the following scenarios: in a classroom learning environment, for academic research, or for contributing to open source projects.
> - For all other usage scenarios: In non-enterprise organizations, up to 5 users can use Visual Studio Community. In enterprise organizations (meaning those with 250 PCs or $1 Million US Dollars in annual revenue), no use is permitted beyond the open source, academic research, and classroom learning environment scenarios described above."

The NORMA plug-in itself can be downloaded as a zip file from SourceForge at http://sourceforge.net/projects/orm/. To download NORMA for an earlier version of Visual Studio (e.g. 2008), click the "NORMA for VisualStudio" folder to show its subfolders, then click the top subfolder (e.g. 2015-01-CTP) to show its subfolders, and then select the relevant zip file. Alternatively, you can download the relevant NORMA zip file from the library section of the ORM Foundation website at http://www.ormfoundation.org/.

The NORMA tool itself is under development at ORM Solutions LLC, whose website (http://ormsolutions.com/) includes access to a web-based viewer for viewing ORM models online.

In addition to NORMA, various other ORM-related tools are available, some free and some commercial. For example, the ActiveFacts tool supports conceptual queries over ORM models using the Constellation Query Language (CQL)—see http://dataconstellation.com/ActiveFacts/index.shtml. Another recently released ORM tool is ORM Studio—see http://viev.com/index.php/products.

Answers

Ex. 1.3

1. Let R be an acyclic relation whose first role is functional (simple uniqueness con-straint). Now populate R with a set of facts that includes the $n-1$ consecutive rela-tionships $a_1Ra_2,\ldots, a_{n-1}Ra_n$. Graphically these $n-1$ relationships form a linear chain with n nodes a_1 through a_n. Since R is acyclic, these n nodes are all distinct from one another. If $n < 3$, the chain is trivially, strongly intransitive. Now consider the non-trivial case where $n \geq 3$, and assume that R is *not* strongly intransitive. Then it is possible to add another R fact that relates a_1 directly to a_n, as shown in red.

    Because of acyclicity, $a_2 \neq a_n$, so element a_1 is now related directly via R to two distinct elements; but this is impossible because of the uniqueness constraint. Hence we cannot make a transitive jump over one or more nodes in the R relation, so the fact type is strongly intransitive.

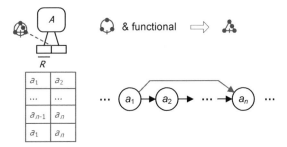

2. If using the bit datatype for Booleans, the constraint may be coded by adding the following check clause to the Employee table:

    check (isChiefExecutiveOfficer = 1 **and** manager **is null**
    　　or
    　　isChiefExecutiveOfficer = 0 **and** manager **is not null**)

    If using the Boolean datatype, the constraint may be coded by adding the following check clause to the Employee table:

    check (isChiefExecutiveOfficer **is true and** manager **is null**
    　　or
    　　isChiefExecutiveOfficer **is false and** manager **is not null**)

Ex. 1.4

1. (a)   C2 violated
   (b)   C4 violated
   (c)   accepted
   (d)   C10 violated
   (e)   C5 (and C6) violated
   (f)   C3 violated
   (g)   C7 violated

2. D

3. (a)   C7 violated
   (b)   C2 violated
   (c)   C1 violated
   (d)   Accepted
   (e)   C3 violated
   (f)   Accepted
   (g)   C8 violated
   (h)   C8 violated
   (i)   Accepted

4. (a)   C7
   (b)   C5

5. (a)

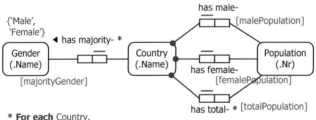

* **For each** Country,
    totalPopulation = malePopulation + femalePopulation.

* **For each** Country:
    majorityGender = 'Male' **if** malePopulation > femalePopulation;
    majorityGender = 'Female' **if** femalePopulation > malePopulation.

3. (b)

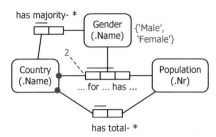

* Country has total- Population$_1$ **iff**
    Country for Gender 'Male' has Population$_2$ **and**
    Country for Gender 'Female' has Population$_3$ **and**
    Population$_1$ = Population$_2$ + Population$_3$.

* Country has majority- Gender 'Male' **if**
    Country for Gender 'Male' has Population$_1$ **and**
    Country for Gender 'Female' has Population$_2$ **and**
    Population$_1$ > Population$_2$.

* Country has majority- Gender 'Female' **if**
    Country for Gender 'Male' has Population$_1$ **and**
    Country for Gender 'Female' has Population$_2$ **and**
    Population$_2$ > Population$_1$.

3. (c)

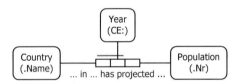

4. (a)

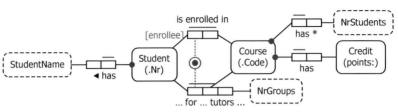

* **For each** Course,
    nrStudents = **count each** Student **who** is enrolled in **that** Course.

aliter: * **For each** Course,
    nrStudents = **count**(enrollee).

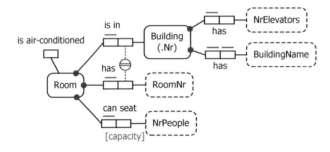

4. (b)

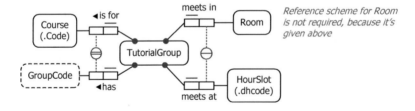

Reference scheme for Room is not required, because it's given above

Ex. 3.1

1.

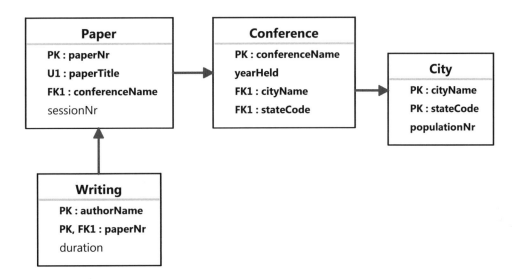

2.

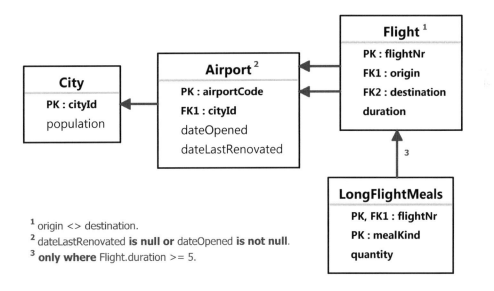

[1] origin <> destination.
[2] dateLastRenovated **is null or** dateOpened **is not null**.
[3] **only where** Flight.duration >= 5.

Ex. 4.1 (Academic Conference)

ORM schema:

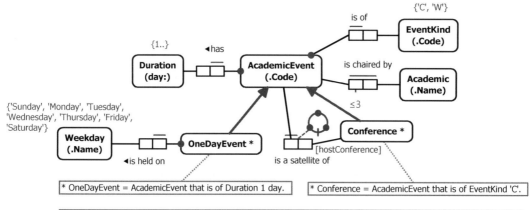

Note: The satellite relationship is functional and acyclic, so is strongly intransitive by implication.

Annotated Relational schema:

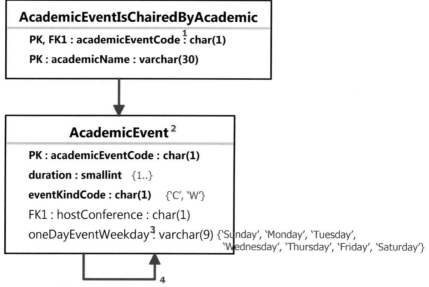

[1] **frequency** <= 3.
[2] (academicEventCode, hostConference) **relationship is acyclic**.
[3] **not null iff** duration = 1.
[4] **only where referenced** academicEventCode **has** eventKindCode 'C'.

Note: To save space, the model report is omitted here.

Ex. 4.2 (Course Prerequisites)

Ex. 4.3 (Concert Bookings)

Part 1:

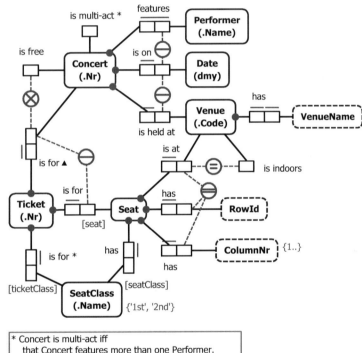

* Concert is multi-act iff
   that Concert features more than one Performer.

* For each Ticket,
   ticketClass = seat.seatClass.

Part 2:

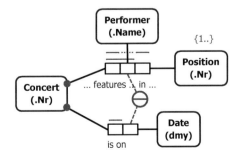

Ex. 4.3 (Concert Bookings)

Part 3:

> * **For each** Venue **that** is indoors,
>   nr1stClassSeats = **count each** Seat **that** is at **that** Venue
>   **and** is of SeatClass '1st'.

Ex. 4.4 (British Monarchs)

Part 1

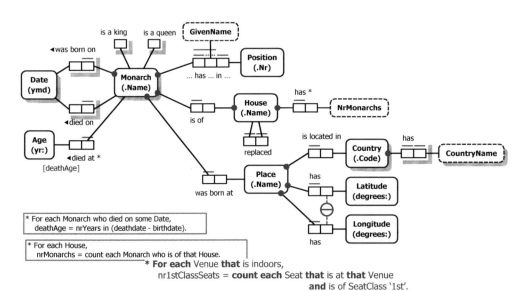

* For each Monarch who died on some Date,
   deathAge = nrYears in (deathdate - birthdate).

* For each House,
   nrMonarchs = count each Monarch who is of that House.

* **For each** Venue **that** is indoors,
    nr1stClassSeats = **count each** Seat **that** is at **that** Venue
                                                        and is of SeatClass '1st'.

Some alternatives:

- Add the injective fact type Place has GridReference, where GridReference is identified by its latitude and longitude.
- Allow mandatory role constraint on birthplace role of Place (I omitted it to allow other places).
- Allow mandatory role constraint on Country role of Place is located in Country (I omitted it to allow other countries and to allow a reference table for countries to be populated before monarch details are added).
- Allow no mandatory role constraint on House role of Monarch is of House (e.g. to discuss other houses).

Ex. 4.4 (British Monarchs)

Part 2

This shows the relevant extensions to the Part 1 schema. Other aspects of the Part 1 schema that have not changed are not repeated here.

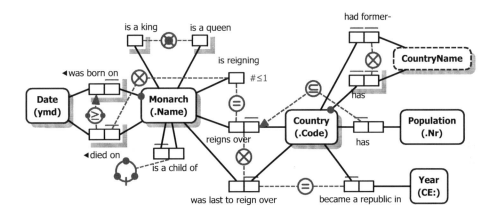

Some alternatives:

- Allow implied mandatory role constraints to be declared explicitly.
- Allow other *reasonable* constraint choices consistent with the data (e.g. simple uniqueness constraints on Monarch's roles in the two reigning-over-country fact types—I omitted these to allow for rare cases where they might not apply). Simple uniqueness constraints on the roles played by Age, Population and Year should *not* be added even though consistent with the data, because they could be violated by future data.

Ex. 4.4 (British Monarchs)

Part 3

Term	Informal Description
House	Official royal family of a British monarch, providing the equivalent of a family name for British monarchs
CountryCode	ISO 3166-1 alpha 2 code for countries as standardized by the International Standards Organization (ISO), e.g. India has the 2-letter ISO 3166-1 code IN. A complete list of the ISO 3166-1 alpha 2 codes is accessible at http://en.wikipedia.org/wiki/ISO_3166-1

Fact Type	Informal Description
Monarch was last to reign over Country	The monarch was the last of those monarchs who previously reigned over the country. The monarch no longer reigns over the country because it has since become a republic.

Verbalization of countryname fact type:

Country has CountryName.
Each Country has **exactly one** CountryName.
For each CountryName, **at most one** Country has **that** CountryName.

Examples:
Country 'AD' has CountryName 'Andorra'.
Country 'AE' has CountryName 'United Arab Emirates'.
Country 'AF' has CountryName 'Afghanistan'.

Sample Constraint Verbalizations:

For each Monarch, **exactly one of the following holds:**
 that Monarch is a king;
 that Monarch is a queen.

For each Country,
 that Country became a republic in **some** Year
 if and only if
 some Monarch was last to reign over **that** Country.

For each Monarch, **at most one of the following holds:**
 that Monarch is reigning;
 that Monarch died on **some** Date.

For each Country,
 if that Country has **some** Population
 then some Monarch reigns over **that** Country.

Annotated Relational Schema:

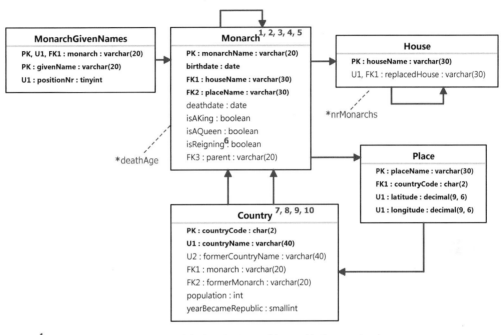

MonarchGivenNames

PK, U1, FK1 : monarch : varchar(20)
PK : givenName : varchar(20)
U1 : positionNr : tinyint

Monarch [1, 2, 3, 4, 5]

PK : monarchName : varchar(20)
birthdate : date
FK1 : houseName : varchar(30)
FK2 : placeName : varchar(30)
deathdate : date
isAKing : boolean
isAQueen : boolean
isReigning [6] : boolean
FK3 : parent : varchar(20)

House

PK : houseName : varchar(30)
U1, FK1 : replacedHouse : varchar(30)

*nrMonarchs

*deathAge

Place

PK : placeName : varchar(30)
FK1 : countryCode : char(2)
U1 : latitude : decimal(9, 6)
U1 : longitude : decimal(9, 6)

Country [7, 8, 9, 10]

PK : countryCode : char(2)
U1 : countryName : varchar(40)
U2 : formerCountryName : varchar(40)
FK1 : monarch : varchar(20)
FK2 : formerMonarch : varchar(20)
population : int
yearBecameRepublic : smallint

[1] (isaKing = **true and** isaQueen = **false**) **or** (isaKing = **false and** isaQueen = **true**).

[2] **existing** deathdate >= birthdate.

[3] deathdate **is null or** (isReigning **is false or** isReigning **is null**).

[4] (monarch, parent) **relationship is acyclic**.

[5] isReigning = **true iff** monarchName **in** Country.monarch.

[6] **count**(isReigning = **true**) <= 1.

[7] monarch ≠ formerMonarch.

[8] formerMonarch **is not null iff** yearBecameRepublic **is not null**.

[9] population **is null or** monarch **is not null**.

[10] countryName **not in** (Country.formerCountryName).

* **For each** Monarch **who** died on **some** Date,
    deathAge = nrYears **in** (deathdate - birthdate).
* **For each** House,
    nrMonarchs = **count each** Monarch **who** is of **that** House.

Notes:

- Allow datatype for latitude to be **decimal**(8,6). While this is strictly more correct, using **decimal**(9,6) allows easier comparison operations between latitude and longitude.
- The derivations may be implemented as computed columns on the Monarch and House tables, or as views.

Ex. 4.5 (Malaysia Database)

Part 1

Main Data page:

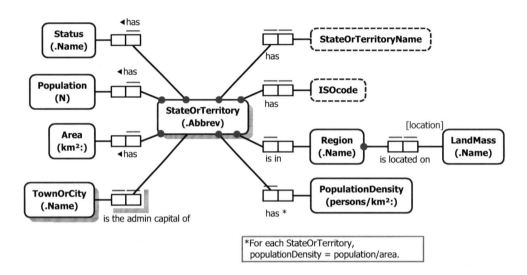

```
*For each StateOrTerritory,
 populationDensity = population/area.
```

ExtraData page:

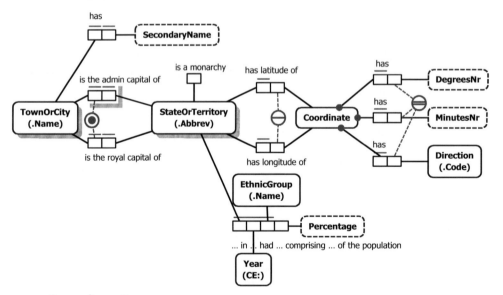

Some alternatives:

- Allow any reasonable replacement of a value type by an entity type, or vice versa, e.g. Population(.Nr) → Population(), Percentage() → Percentage(.Nr), DegreesNr() → Degrees(.Nr), MinutesNr() → Minutes(.Nr),
- Allow mandatory role constraint on other role played by Region (optionality allows entry of location facts first).
- Allow StateOrTerritory is located on LandMass, instead of StateOrTerritory is located in Region (because 1:1).
- Allow any clear formulation of the derivation rule (formal syntax not required).
- Allow equivalent forms obtained by nesting/co-referencing/flattening, e.g. the quaternary may be nested by objectifying of StateOrTerritory in Year has EthnicGroup as EthnicComponent, and adding the mandatory, *n:*1 fact type EthnicComponent occurs in Percentage. The binary fact type for Status may be replaced by two unaries: StateOrTerritory is a state, StateOrTerritory is a territory.

Ex. 4.5 (Malaysia Database)

Part 2

StateOrTerritory:

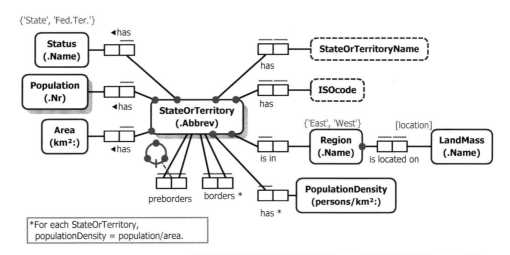

*For each StateOrTerritory,
  populationDensity = population/area.

X preborders Y iff X and Y are neighbors, and the abbreviation identifying X is alphabetically before that of Y.

*StateOrTerritory1 borders StateOrTerritory2 iff
StateOrTerritory1 preborders StateOrTerritory2
or
StateOrTerritory2 preborders StateOrTerritory1.

The following textual constraint implies, and is more efficient than, the acyclic constraint:
  If StateOrTerritory1 preborders StateOrTerritory2
  then StateOrTerritory1.abbrev < StateOrTerritory2.abbrev.

Irreflexive is implied for borders predicate.

SubtypingEtc:

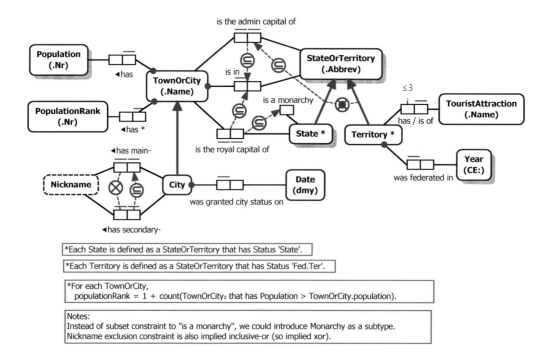

*Each State is defined as a StateOrTerritory that has Status 'State'.

*Each Territory is defined as a StateOrTerritory that has Status 'Fed.Ter.'.

*For each TownOrCity,
  populationRank = 1 + count(TownOrCity₂ that has Population > TownOrCity.population).

Notes:
Instead of subset constraint to "is a monarchy", we could introduce Monarchy as a subtype.
Nickname exclusion constraint is also implied inclusive-or (so implied xor).

ExtraStateData:

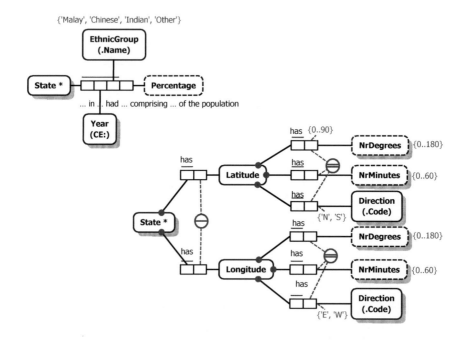

Ex. 4.5 (Malaysia Database)

Part 3

Term	Informal Description
EthnicGroup	Major racial or ethnic group (e.g. Chinese).
ISOcode	ISO 3166-2 code for states/provinces/regions within countries as standardized by the International Standards Organization (ISO), e.g. Johor has the ISO code MY-01. A full list of ISO 3166-2 codes is accessible at http://www.commondatahub.com/live/geography/state_province_region/iso_3166_2_state_codes.
PopulationRank	A city or town's rank based on the size of its population. A rank of 1 indicates the largest population. The larger the rank number, the smaller the population.
StateOrTerritory	A major subdivision of a country. Either a State or a Federal Territory.

Fact Type	Informal Description and Sample Population
StateOrTerritory preborders StateOrTerritory	StateOrTerritory$_1$ preborders StateOrTerritory$_2$ if and only if StateOrTerritory$_1$ borders StateOrTerritory$_2$ and the abbreviation of StateOrTerritory$_1$ is alphabetically prior to the abbreviation of StateOrTerritory$_2$. **Examples:** StateOrTerritory 'JHR' preborders StateOrTerritory 'NSN'. StateOrTerritory 'JHR' preborders StateOrTerritory 'PHG'. StateOrTerritory 'NSN' preborders StateOrTerritory 'PHG'. (JHN = Johor, NSN = Negeri Sembilan, PHG = Pahang)

Sample Constraint Verbalizations:

If some TownOrCity is the admin capital of **some** StateOrTerritory

then that TownOrCity is in **that** StateOrTerritory.

If some City has **some** secondary Nickname **then that** City has **some** main Nickname.

For each Nickname, **at most one of the following holds:**

    some City has **that** main Nickname;

    some City has **that** secondary Nickname.

Each City has **at most** 3 **instances of** TouristAttraction.

No StateOrTerritory **may cycle back to itself via one or more traversals through**

    StateOrTerritory preborders StateOrTerritory

Annotated relational schema:

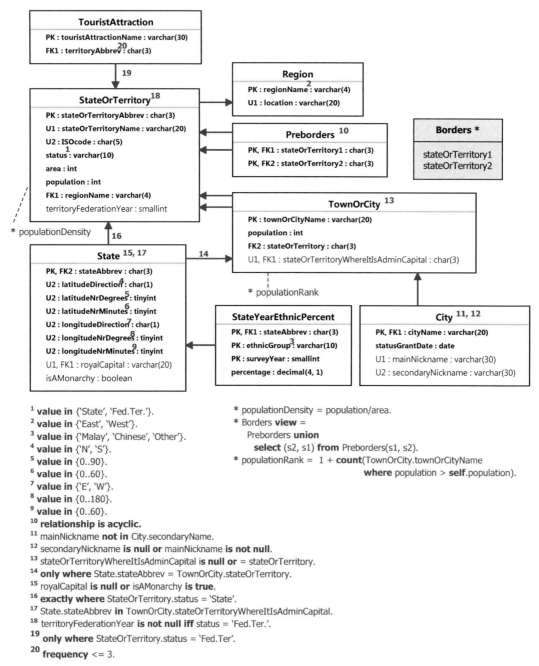

TouristAttraction

PK : touristAttractionName : varchar(30)
FK1 : territoryAbbrev[20] : char(3)

19

StateOrTerritory[18]

PK : stateOrTerritoryAbbrev : char(3)
U1 : stateOrTerritoryName : varchar(20)
U2 : ISOcode : char(5)
status[1] : varchar(10)
area : int
population : int
FK1 : regionName : varchar(4)
territoryFederationYear : smallint

* populationDensity

Region

PK : regionName[2] : varchar(4)
U1 : location : varchar(20)

Preborders 10

PK, FK1 : stateOrTerritory1 : char(3)
PK, FK2 : stateOrTerritory2 : char(3)

Borders *

stateOrTerritory1
stateOrTerritory2

TownOrCity 13

PK : townOrCityName : varchar(20)
population : int
FK2 : stateOrTerritory : char(3)
U1, FK1 : stateOrTerritoryWhereItIsAdminCapital : char(3)

* populationRank

16

State 15, 17

PK, FK2 : stateAbbrev : char(3)
U2 : latitudeDirection[4] : char(1)
U2 : latitudeNrDegrees[5] : tinyint
U2 : latitudeNrMinutes[6] : tinyint
U2 : longitudeDirection[7] : char(1)
U2 : longitudeNrDegrees[8] : tinyint
U2 : longitudeNrMinutes[9] : tinyint
U1, FK1 : royalCapital : varchar(20)
isAMonarchy : boolean

14

StateYearEthnicPercent

PK, FK1 : stateAbbrev : char(3)
PK : ethnicGroup[3] : varchar(10)
PK : surveyYear : smallint
percentage : decimal(4, 1)

City 11, 12

PK, FK1 : cityName : varchar(20)
statusGrantDate : date
U1 : mainNickname : varchar(30)
U2 : secondaryNickname : varchar(30)

[1] **value in** {'State', 'Fed.Ter.'}.
[2] **value in** {'East', 'West'}.
[3] **value in** {'Malay', 'Chinese', 'Other'}.
[4] **value in** {'N', 'S'}.
[5] **value in** {0..90}.
[6] **value in** {0..60}.
[7] **value in** {'E', 'W'}.
[8] **value in** {0..180}.
[9] **value in** {0..60}.
[10] **relationship is acyclic.**
[11] mainNickname **not in** City.secondaryName.
[12] secondaryNickname **is null or** mainNickname **is not null**.
[13] stateOrTerritoryWhereItIsAdminCapital **is null or** = stateOrTerritory.
[14] **only where** State.stateAbbrev = TownOrCity.stateOrTerritory.
[15] royalCapital **is null or** isAMonarchy **is true**.
[16] **exactly where** StateOrTerritory.status = 'State'.
[17] State.stateAbbrev **in** TownOrCity.stateOrTerritoryWhereItIsAdminCapital.
[18] territoryFederationYear **is not null iff** status = 'Fed.Ter.'.
[19] **only where** StateOrTerritory.status = 'Fed.Ter'.
[20] **frequency** <= 3.

* populationDensity = population/area.
* Borders **view** =
    Preborders **union**
        select (s2, s1) **from** Preborders(s1, s2).
* populationRank = 1 + **count**(TownOrCity.townOrCityName
                                where population > **self**.population).

Notes: Adding the constraint stateOrTerritory1 < stateOrTerritory2 to the Preborders table implies (and is more efficient than) the acyclic constraint. A reduction transform allows the stateOrTerritoryWhereItIsAdminCapital attribute to be replaced by the Boolean attribute isAdminCapital.

Ex. 4.6 (Nobel Prize Awards)

Part 1

Q. 1

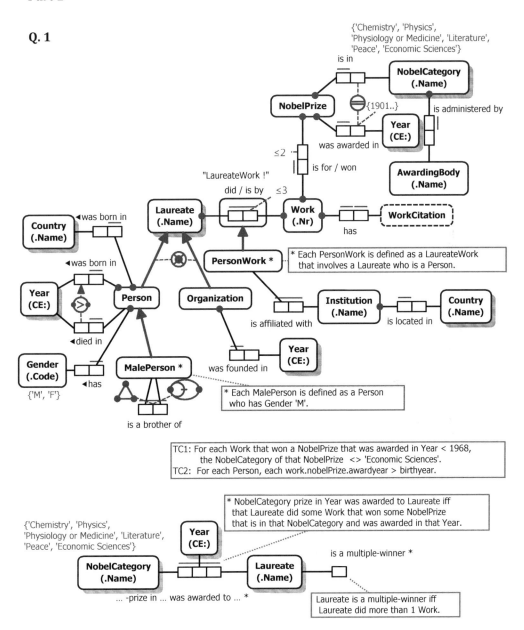

TC1: For each Work that won a NobelPrize that was awarded in Year < 1968,
the NobelCategory of that NobelPrize <> 'Economic Sciences'.
TC2: For each Person, each work.nobelPrize.awardyear > birthyear.

Note: Textual constraint TC2 can be declared graphically as a value-comparison constraint
with a specified join path in the professional version of NORMA.

Q. 2

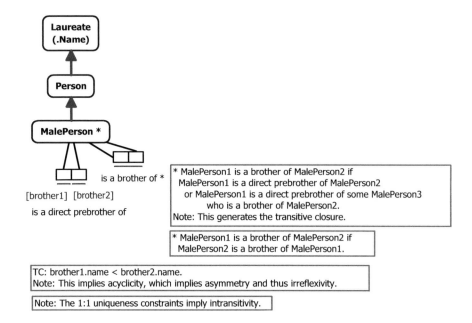

The derivation for the brotherhood relation is declared above using two recursive rules. This derivation may also be expressed as a single derivation rule using disjunction.

X is a direct prebrother of Y means that X and Y are brothers where the name of X is alphabetically directly before the name of Y.

As an alternative to the textual constraint on the direct prebrotherhood fact type, you can declare an acyclic constraint. Since the predicate is also functional, this implies strong intransitivity. For relational implementation, the textual constraint is more efficient.

Other solutions are possible (e.g. using semiderivation). The solution should enable brotherhood facts for a set of *n* brothers to be asserted using just *n*-1 facts, while enabling the derivation of all other brotherhood facts. For example, for 4 brothers ordered by name as *a, b, c, d* we assert just 3 facts *aBb, bBc, cBd* and derive *aBc, aBd, bBd* and the converses of these 6 facts, yielding 12 facts.

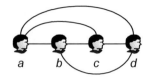

Ex. 4.6 (Nobel Prize Awards)

Part 2

Term	Informal Description
Laureate	*Person or organization that won a Nobel prize.*
Work	*Activity performed that merits consideration for a Nobel prize.*
LaureateWork	*Performance of a specific work by a specific laureate.*

Fact Type	Informal Description and Sample Population
NobelCategory is administered by AwardingBody	*A nobel category is administered by an awarding body if that body is responsible for granting the awards in that category.* **Examples:** NobelCategory 'Physics' is administered by AwardingBody 'The Royal Swedish Academy'. NobelCategory 'Chemistry' is administered by AwardingBody 'The Royal Swedish Academy'. NobelCategory 'Peace' is administered by AwardingBody 'The Norwegain Nobel Committee'.

Sample Constraint Verbalizations:

Each NobelPrize is for **at most** 2 **instances of** Work.

For each NobelCategory **and** Year,
 at most one NobelPrize is in **that** NobelCategory **and** was awarded in **that** Year.
This association with NobelCategory, Year **provides the preferred identification scheme for** NobelPrize.

For each Laureate, **exactly one of the following holds:**
 that Laureate is **some** Organization;
 that Laureate is **some** Person.

If MalePerson$_1$ is a brother of MalePerson$_2$
 and MalePerson$_2$ is a brother of MalePerson$_3$
 then MalePerson$_1$ is a brother of MalePerson$_3$.

If MalePerson$_1$ is a brother of MalePerson$_2$
 then MalePerson$_2$ is a brother of MalePerson$_1$.
No MalePerson is a brother of **the same** MalePerson.

Annotated relational schema:

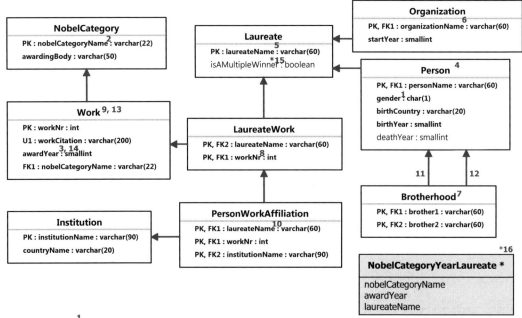

1 **value in** {'M', 'F'}.

2 **value in** {'Chemistry', 'Physics', 'Physiology or Medicine', 'Literature', 'Peace', 'Economic Sciences'}.

3 **value** >= 1901.

4 **existing** deathYear > birthYear.

5 = (Organization.organizationName **union** Person.personName.

6 **not in** Person.personName.

7 **relationship is irreflexive, symmetric** and **transitive**.

8 **frequency** <= 3.

9 (nobelCategoryName, awardYear) **frequency** <= 2.

10 **in** Person.personName.

11 **only where** Person.gender = 'M'.

12 **only where** Person.gender = 'M'.

13 awardYear >= 1968 **or** nobelCategoryName <> 'Economic Sciences'.

14 > (Work **natural join** LaureateWork **join** Person **on** laureateName = personName).birthYear.

*15 = **true iff** laureateName **in** (LaureateWork.laureateName **having count**(workNr) > 1).

*16 = (Work **natural join** LaureateWork)/[nobelCategoryName, awardYear, laureateName].

Ex. 4.7 (Academy Awards)

Part 1

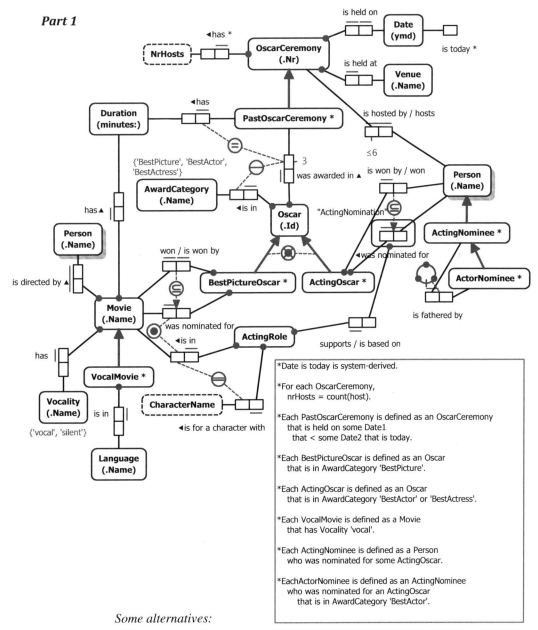

*Date is today is system-derived.

*For each OscarCeremony,
  nrHosts = count(host).

*Each PastOscarCeremony is defined as an OscarCeremony
    that is held on some Date1
        that < some Date2 that is today.

*Each BestPictureOscar is defined as an Oscar
    that is in AwardCategory 'BestPicture'.

*Each ActingOscar is defined as an Oscar
    that is in AwardCategory 'BestActor' or 'BestActress'.

*Each VocalMovie is defined as a Movie
    that has Vocality 'vocal'.

*Each ActingNominee is defined as a Person
    who was nominated for some ActingOscar.

*EachActorNominee is defined as an ActingNominee
    who was nominated for an ActingOscar
        that is in AwardCategory 'BestActor'.

Some alternatives:
- Derive OscarCeremony is past and use it to define PastOscarCeremony.
- Instead of the subtype ActingNominee, use Person is the father of Person, with a subset constraint from each role to the nominee role in Person was nominated for ActingOscar.
- Objectification may be replaced by coreferencing.

Ex. 4.7 (Academy Awards)

Part 2

Term	Informal Description
ActingRole	*Character played within a specific movie.*
Vocality	*Property of a movie that classifies it as either spoken or silent.*

Fact Type	Informal Description
OscarCeremony is hosted by Person	*An Oscar ceremony is hosted by a person if that person is on stage at the ceremony to manage and introduce the award presentations.*

Sample Fact Type Verbalization with Sample Population:

OscarCeremony is held at Venue.
Each OscarCeremony is held at **exactly one** Venue.
It is possible that more than one OscarCeremony is held at **the same** Venue.

Examples:
OscarCeremony 1 is held at Venue 'Hollywood Roosevelt Hotel'.
OscarCeremony 2 is held at Venue 'Ambassador Hotel'.
OscarCeremony 3 is held at Venue 'Ambassador Hotel'.

Sample Constraint Verbalizations:

Each OscarCeremony is hosted by **at most** 6 **instances of** Person.

For each PastOscarCeremony,
  that PastOscarCeremony has **some** Duration **if and only if**
  some Oscar was awarded in **that** PastOscarCeremony.

If some Movie won **some** BestPictureOscar
then that Movie was nominated for **that** BestPictureOscar.

No ActingNominee **may cycle back to itself via one or more traversals through**
  ActingNominee is fathered by ActingNominee.

Annotated relational schema:

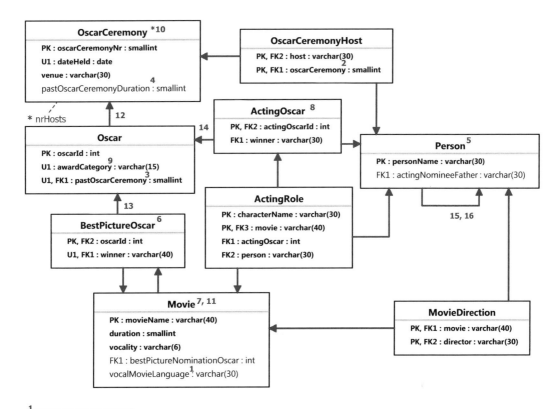

¹ **value in** {'vocal', 'silent'}.

² **frequency** <= 6.

³ **frequency** = 3.

⁴ **not null iff** oscarCeremonyNr **in** Oscar.pastOscarCeremony.

⁵ **relationship is acyclic**.

⁶ (oscarId, winner) **in** Movie.(bestPictureNominationOscar, movieName).

⁷ bestPictureNominationOscar **is not null or** movieName **in** ActingRole.movie..

⁸ (actingOscarId, winner) **in** ActingRole.(actingOscar, person).

⁹ **value in** {'BestPicture', 'BestActro', 'BestActress'}.

^{* 10} nrHosts = **count**(host) **from** OscarCeremony
                   where oscarCeremony = **self**.oscarCeremonyNr.

¹¹ vocalMovieLanguage **is not null iff** vocality = 'vocal'.

¹² **only where** dateHeld < **today**.

¹³ **exactly where referencing** oscarId **in** Oscar.oscarId **where** awardCategory = 'BestPicture'.

¹⁴ **exactly where** actingOscarId **in** Oscar.oscarId **where** awardCategory **in** {'BestActor', 'BestActress'}.

¹⁵ **only where referencing** personName **in** ActingRole.person.

¹⁶ **only where referenced** personName **in** ActingRole.person
                   where actingOscar **in** Oscar.oscarId **where** awardCategory = 'BestActor'.

Ex. 5.1

1. (a)

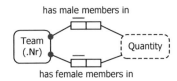

(b) Without further assumptions, the schema transforms as shown opposite.

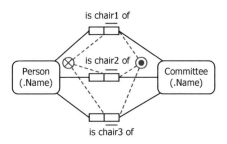

If we assume that chair1 is selected before any other chairs, we may strengthen the solution as shown opposite.

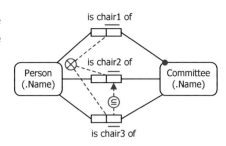

(c)

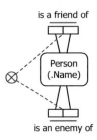

(d)

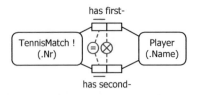

Ex. 5.1

2.

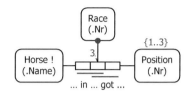

3. (a)

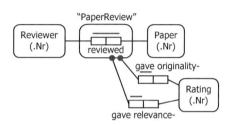

(b)

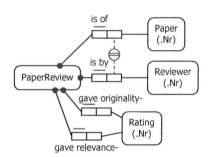

4.

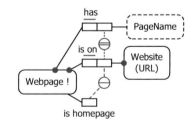

5.

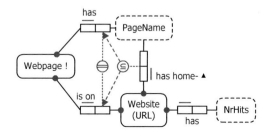

Ex. 5.2

1.

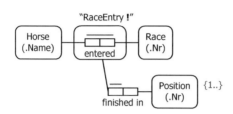

aliter: Use co-referencing instead of nesting.

2. (a)   9 tables.

(b)

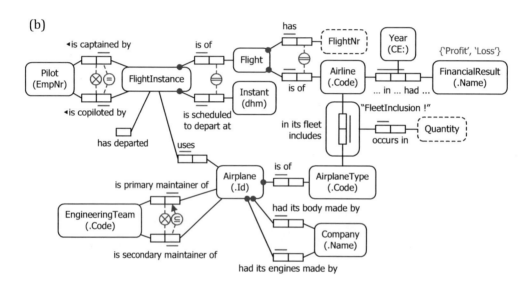

(c) 4 tables

(d)   *AirlineYear* (airlineCode, yr, financialResult)
{Profit, Loss}

FleetInclusion (airlineCode, airplaneType, [quantity])

FlightInstance (airlineCode, flightNr, scheduledDeparture, [captain, copilot], departed, [airplaneId])

Airplane (airplaneId, airplaneType, bodyManufacturer, engineManufacturer,
[maintenanceTeam1, [maintenanceTeam2]])

Ex. 5.4 (Solar System Exercise)

Part 1:

1. **Discovery** has a functional dependency (bodyName → yearDiscovered) from just part of the key (bodyName, discoverer), allowing redundant instances of the fact type SolarBody was discovered in Year. For example, the fact that Eris was discovered in 2005 appears 3 times (once for each discoverer).

    Atmosphere has the declared primary key (bodyName, gasFormula) as well as an undeclared alternate key (bodyName, gasName). Atmosphere has functional dependencies (gasFormula → gasName and gasName → gasFormula) from just part of a key, allowing redundant instances of the fact type Gas(.formula) has GasName() (e.g. the fact that the gas with formula 'CH4' has the name 'methane' appears 4 times).

2.

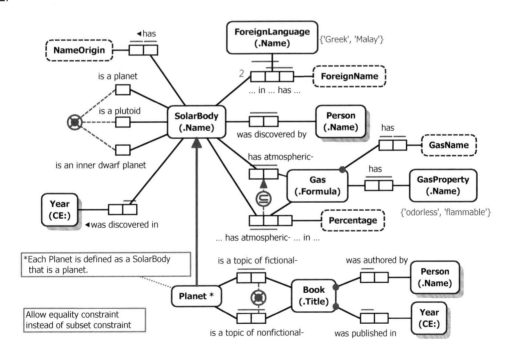

Note: The data type of author should be **nvarchar**(30) to allow Person for author and discoverer.

Ex. 5.4 (Solar System Exercise: Part 1)

3. (a)

```
select distinct SolarBody.bodyName,
case
 when isPlanet = 1 then 'Planet'
 when isPlutoid = 1 then 'Plutoid'
 else 'InnerDwarfPlanet'    -- aliter: when isInnerDwarfPlanet = 1 then
'InnerDwarfPlanet'
end as bodytype,
yearDiscovered
from SolarBody left outer join Discovery
  on SolarBody.bodyName = Discovery.bodyName
```

bodyName	bodytype	yearDiscovered
Ceres	InnerDwarfPlanet	1801
Earth	Planet	NULL
Eris	Plutoid	2005
Haumea	Plutoid	2003
Jupiter	Planet	NULL
Makemake	Plutoid	2005
Mars	Planet	NULL
Mercury	Planet	NULL
Neptune	Planet	1846
Pluto	Plutoid	1930
Saturn	Planet	NULL
Uranus	Planet	1781
Venus	Planet	NULL

(13 ow(s) affected)

3. (b)

```
select SolarBody.bodyName, nameOrigin, Greek.foreignName as greekName,
      Malay.foreignName as malayName
from SolarBody left outer join ForeignNames as Greek
    on SolarBody.bodyName = Greek.bodyName
        and Greek.foreignLanguage = 'Greek'
        left outer join ForeignNames as Malay
          on SolarBody.bodyName = Malay.bodyName
              and Malay.foreignLanguage = 'Malay'
```

bodyName	nameOrigin	greekName	malayName
Ceres	Roman goddess of the harvest	NULL	NULL
Earth	NULL	Gaea	Bumi
Eris	Greek goddess of discord	NULL	NULL
Haumea	Hawaiian goddess of fertility	NULL	NULL
Jupiter	Roman king of the gods	NULL	NULL
Mars	Roman god of war	Ares	Marikh
Mercury	Roman messenger god	Hermes	Utarid
Neptune	Roman god of the sea	Poseidon	Neptun
Pluto	Roman god of the underworld	Pluto	Pluto
Saturn	Roman god of agriculture	Kronos	Zuhal
Uranus	Roman sky god	Uranos	Uranus
Venus	Roman god of love	Aphrodite	Zuhrah

(13 row(s) affected)

Ex. 5.4 (Solar System Exercise: Part 1)

3. (c)

```
select bodyName, FictionBookTopic.bookTitle, author, 'fiction' as bookType
from FictionBookTopic join Book
  on FictionBookTopic.bookTitle = Book.bookTitle
union
select bodyName, NonFictionBookTopic.bookTitle, author, 'nonfiction' as
bookType
from NonFictionBookTopic join Book
  on NonFictionBookTopic.bookTitle = Book.bookTitle
union
select bodyName, null as bookTitle, null as author, null as bookType
from SolarBody
where isPlanet =1
  and bodyName not in(select bodyName from FictionBookTopic)
  and bodyName not in(select bodyName from NonFictionBookTopic)
```

bodyName	bookTitle	author	bookType
Earth	Melbourne and Mars	Joseph Frazer	fiction
Earth	The War of the Worlds	H. G. Wells	fiction
Jupiter	Jupiter: A Novel (Grand Tour)	Ben Bova	fiction
Mars	A Princess of Mars	Edgar Rice Burroughs	fiction
Mars	Melbourne and Mars	Joseph Frazer	fiction
Mars	The Gods of Mars	Edgar Rice Burroughs	fiction
Mars	The War of the Worlds	H. G. Wells	fiction
Earth	Mission to Mars	Michael Collins	nonfiction
Mars	Mars: a Cosmic Stepping Stone	Kevin Nolan	nonfiction
Mars	Mission to Mars	Michael Collins	nonfiction
Mercury	NULL	NULL	NULL
Neptune	NULL	NULL	NULL
Saturn	NULL	NULL	NULL
Uranus	NULL	NULL	NULL
Venus	NULL	NULL	NULL

(15 row(s) affected)

Ex. 5.4 (Solar System Exercise: Part 2)

1. *The ORM schema after performing five optimization transforms:*

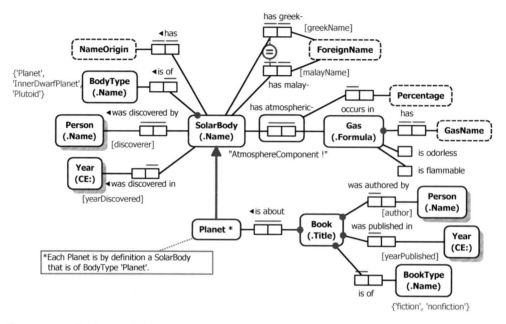

2. *The annotated relational schema:*

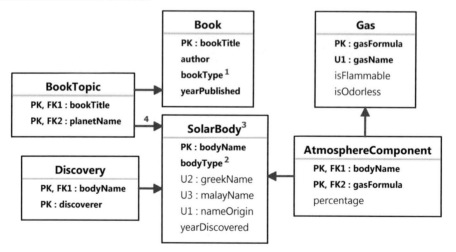

[1] **value in** {'fiction', 'nonfiction'}.

[2] **value in** {'Planet', 'InnerDwarfPlanet', 'Plutoid'}.

[3] greekName **is not null iff** malayName **is not null**.

[4] **only where** SolarBody.bodyType = 'Planet'.

Ex. 5.4 (Solar System Exercise: Part 3)

1.   Populate Book before BookTopic.

Populate SolarBody before BookTopic, Discovery and AtmosphereComponent.

Populate Gas before AtmosphereComponent.

```
use SolarBody1       -- Note: may omit "as booktype" below

insert into SolarBody2DB.dbo.Book
select Book.bookTitle, author, 'fiction' as bookType, yearPublished
from Book join FictionBookTopic
   on Book.bookTitle = FictionBookTopic.bookTitle
union
select Book.bookTitle, author, 'nonfiction' as bookType,
yearPublished
from Book join NonFictionBookTopic
   on Book.bookTitle = NonFictionBookTopic.bookTitle


bookTitle               author          bookType  yearPublished
----------------------- --------------------------- ------------- -------------
A Princess of Mars        Edgar Rice Burroughs  fiction      1917
Jupiter: A Novel (Grand Tour) Ben Bova       fiction        2002
Mars: a Cosmic Stepping Stone Kevin Nolan    nonfiction     2007
Melbourne and Mars        Joseph Frazer    fiction      1889
Mission to Mars          Michael Collins   nonfiction    1990
The Gods of Mars         Edgar Rice Burroughs  fiction      1918
The War of the Worlds    H. G. Wells       fiction      1898

(7 row(s) affected)


insert into SolarBody2DB.dbo.SolarBody
select distinct SolarBody.bodyName,
case
 when isPlanet = 1 then 'Planet'
 when isPlutoid = 1 then 'Plutoid'
 else 'InnerDwarfPlanet'
end as bodytype,                  -- may omit "as bodytype"
Greek.foreignName as greekName,
Malay.foreignName as malayName,
nameOrigin,
yearDiscovered
from SolarBody left outer join ForeignNames as Greek
   on SolarBody.bodyName = Greek.bodyName
     and Greek.foreignLanguage = 'Greek'
 left outer join ForeignNames as Malay
   on SolarBody.bodyName = Malay.bodyName
     and Malay.foreignLanguage = 'Malay'
 left outer join Discovery
   on SolarBody.bodyName = Discovery.bodyName
```

```
bodyName     bodyType          greekName   malayName   nameOrigin                        yearDiscovered
-----------  ----------------  ----------  ----------  --------------------------------  --------------
Ceres        InnerDwarfPlanet  NULL        NULL        Roman goddess of the harvest      1801
Earth        Planet            Gaea        Bumi        NULL                              NULL
Eris         Plutoid           NULL        NULL        Greek goddess of discord          2005
Haumea       Plutoid           NULL        NULL        Hawaiian goddess of fertility     2003
Jupiter      Planet            Zeus        Musytari    Roman king of the gods            NULL
Makemake     Plutoid           NULL        NULL        Rapanui creator of humanity       2005
Mars         Planet            Ares        Marikh      Roman god of war                  NULL
Mercury      Planet            Hermes      Utarid      Roman messenger god               NULL
Neptune      Planet            Poseidon    Neptun      Roman god of the sea              1846
Pluto        Plutoid           Pluto       Pluto       Roman god of the underworld       1930
Saturn       Planet            Kronos      Zuhal       Roman god of agriculture          NULL
Uranus       Planet            Uranos      Uranus      Roman sky god                     1781
Venus        Planet            Aphrodite   Zuhrah      Roman god of love                 NULL

(13 row(s) affected)
```

```
        insert into SolarBody2DB.dbo.Gas
        select distinct gasFormula, gasName,
        case
         when gasFormula in
              (select gasFormula from GasProperty where property =
        'flammable')
         then 1
         else 0
        end as isFlammable,              -- may omit "as isFlammable"
        case
         when gasFormula in
              (select gasFormula from GasProperty where property =
        'odorless')
              then 1
         else 0
        end as isOdorless                -- may omit "as isOdorless"
        from Atmosphere
```

```
        gasFormula gasName                isFlammable isOdorless
        ---------- --------------------   ----------- ----------
        Ar         argon                      0           1
        CH4        methane                    1           1
        CO         carbon monoxide            1           1
        CO2        carbon dioxide             0           1
        H2         hydrogen                   1           1
        He         helium                     0           1
        N2         nitrogen                   0           1
        O2         oxygen                     0           1
        SO2        sulfur dioxide             0           0

        (9 row(s) affected)
```

```
        insert into SolarBody2DB.dbo.AtmosphereComponent
        select * from AtmospherePercent
```

```
        bodyName    gasFormula      percentage
        ----------- ----------  ----------------------------------------
        Earth       Ar              0.930
        Earth       CO2             0.040
        Earth       N2             78.000
        Earth       O2             21.000
        Jupiter     CH4             0.300
        Jupiter     H2             89.800
        Jupiter     He             10.200
```

```
Mars          Ar                    1.600
Mars          CO                    0.080
Mars          CO2                  95.300
Mars          N2                    2.700
Mars          O2                    0.130
Mercury       CO                    0.080
Mercury       H2                   22.000
Mercury       He                    6.000
Mercury       O2                   42.000
Neptune       CH4                   1.500
Neptune       H2                   80.000
Neptune       He                   18.000
Pluto         N2                   90.000
Saturn        CH4                   0.400
Saturn        H2                   96.000
Saturn        He                    3.000
Uranus        CH4                   2.300
Uranus        H2                   83.000
Uranus        He                   15.000
Venus         CO2                  96.500
Venus         N2                    3.500
Venus         SO2                   0.015

(29 row(s) affected)

insert into SolarBody2DB.dbo.BookTopic
select bookTitle, bodyName as planetName        -- may omit "as planetName"
from FictionBookTopic
union
select bookTitle, bodyName as planetName        -- may omit "as planetName"
from NonFictionBookTopic
order by bookTitle

bookTitle                        planetName
-------------------------------  ----------------
A Princess of Mars               Mars
Jupiter: A Novel (Grand Tour)    Jupiter
Mars: a Cosmic Stepping Stone    Mars
Melbourne and Mars               Earth
Melbourne and Mars               Mars
Mission to Mars                  Earth
Mission to Mars                  Mars
The Gods of Mars                 Mars
The War of the Worlds            Earth
The War of the Worlds            Mars

(10 row(s) affected)

insert into SolarBody2DB.dbo.Discovery
select bodyName, discoverer
from Discovery




bodyName        discoverer
--------------- -----------------------------
Ceres           Guiseppe Piazzi
Eris            Chad Trujillo
Eris            David Rabinowitz
```

```
Eris            Michael Brown
Haumea          ???
Makemake        Chad Trujillo
Makemake        David Rabinowitz
Makemake        Micheal Brown
Neptune         Johan Gottfried Galle
Neptune         John Couch Adams
Neptune         Urbain Le Verrier
Pluto           Clyde Tombaugh
Uranus          William Herschel

(13 row(s) affected)
```

2. (a)

```
use SolarBody2DB

select bodyName, bodyType, yearDiscovered
from SolarBody
```

bodyName	bodyType	yearDiscovered
Ceres	InnerDwarfPlanet	1801
Earth	Planet	NULL
Eris	Plutoid	2005
Haumea	Plutoid	2003
Jupiter	Planet	NULL
Makemake	Plutoid	2005
Mars	Planet	NULL
Mercury	Planet	NULL
Neptune	Planet	1846
Pluto	Plutoid	1930
Saturn	Planet	NULL
Uranus	Planet	1781
Venus	Planet	NULL

(13 row(s) affected)

(b)

```
select bodyName, nameOrigin, greekName, malayName
from SolarBody
```

bodyName	nameOrigin	greekName	malayName
Ceres	Roman goddess of the harvest	NULL	NULL
Earth	NULL	Gaea	Bumi
Eris	Greek goddess of discord	NULL	NULL
Haumea	Hawaiian goddess of fertility	NULL	NULL
Jupiter	Roman king of the gods	Zeus	Musytari
Makemake	Rapanui creator of humanity	NULL	NULL
Mars	Roman god of war	Ares	Marikh
Mercury	Roman messenger god	Hermes	Utarid
Neptune	Roman god of the sea	Poseidon	Neptun
Pluto	Roman god of the underworld	Pluto	Pluto
Saturn	Roman god of agriculture	Kronos	Zuhal
Uranus	Roman sky god	Uranos	Uranus
Venus	Roman god of love	Aphrodite	Zuhrah

(13 row(s) affected)

(c)
```
select SolarBody.bodyName, BookTopic.bookTitle, author, bookType
from SolarBody left outer join (BookTopic join Book
                        on Book.bookTitle = BookTopic.bookTitle)
   on SolarBody.bodyName = BookTopic.planetName
where bodyType = 'Planet'
```

bodyName	bookTitle	author	bookType
Earth	Melbourne and Mars	Joseph Frazer	fiction
Earth	Mission to Mars	Michael Collins	nonfiction
Earth	The War of the Worlds	H. G. Wells	fiction
Jupiter	Jupiter: A Novel (Grand Tour)	Ben Bova	fiction
Mars	A Princess of Mars	Edgar Rice Burroughs	fiction
Mars	Mars: a Cosmic Stepping Stone	Kevin Nolan	nonfiction
Mars	Melbourne and Mars	Joseph Frazer	fiction
Mars	Mission to Mars	Michael Collins	nonfiction
Mars	The Gods of Mars	Edgar Rice Burroughs	fiction
Mars	The War of the Worlds	H. G. Wells	fiction
Mercury	NULL	NULL	NULL
Neptune	NULL	NULL	NULL
Saturn	NULL	NULL	NULL
Uranus	NULL	NULL	NULL
Venus	NULL	NULL	NULL

```
    (15 row(s) affected)
```

Ex. 6.1

1.   Person is a rigid type so cannot be a subtype of a role type such as Lecturer.

2.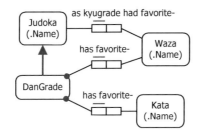

3.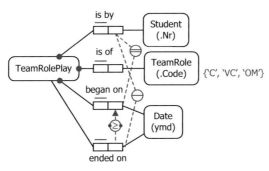

4.

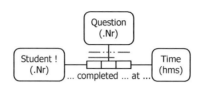

5.   Two solutions are shown below. The first solution assumes that on any given date a person can start (or end) at most one of these roles (Teacher or Researcher). The second solution allows that someone could start (or end) both roles on the same date.

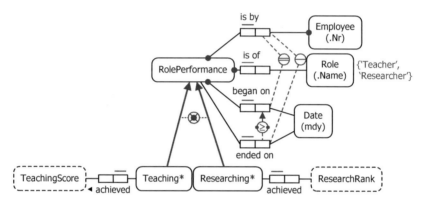

*Each Teaching **is defined as a** RolePerformance **that** is of Role 'Teaching'.
*Each Researching **is defined as a** RolePerformance **that** is of Role 'Researcher'.

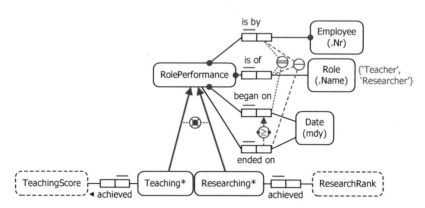

*Each Teaching **is defined as a** RolePerformance **that** is of Role 'Teaching'.
*Each Researching **is defined as a** RolePerformance **that** is of Role 'Researcher'.

Ex. 6.2

1.   B

2.

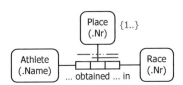

3.

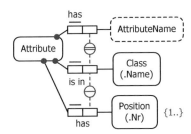

4.

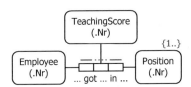

Index

A

acyclic, 8, 140
acyclic constraint, 8
alethic constraint, 9, 28
alethic modality, 28
annotated relational schema, 56
arity, 28
asserted fact, 28
asserted fact type, 28
asserted subtype, 28, 36
atomic fact, 2, 28
    elementary fact, 2
    existential fact, 2
atomic fact type, 28

B

bag, 129
binary, 1, 134
business domain, 1

C

collection types, 128
Conceptual Schema Design Procedure (CSDP), 2
conceptual schema optimization, 98
constraint, 6
    acyclic constraint, 6
    alethic constraint, 6
    deontic constraint, 6
    exclusion constraint, 6
    exclusive-or constraint, 6
    external frequency constraint, 6
    external uniqueness constraint, 6
    inclusive-or constraint, 6
    internal frequency constraint, 6
    internal uniqueness constraint, 6
    join subset constraint, 6
    locally reflexive, 6
    mandatory role constraint, 6
    object cardinality constraint, 6
    object type value constraint, 6
    ring constraint, 6
    role cardinality constraint, 6
    strongly intransitive, 6
    subset constraint, 6
    subtyping constraints, 6
    symmetric, 6
    textual constraint, 6
    transitive, 6
    uniqueness constraint, 6
    value-comparison constraint, 6
coreferencing, 91
counterexample, 6

D

data migration, 108
data modeling patterns, 119
data type, 10
data use case, 2, 3
data value, 3
deontic constraint, 141
derivation rule, 8, 138
derived fact type, 8, 138
derived subtype, 36
disjunctive mandatory role constraint. *See*
    inclusive-or constraint
domain value, 3

E

eager evaluation, 138
elementary fact, 2
entity, 3
entity type, 5, 133
equality constraint, 137
event, 120
    once-only event, 120
    period event, 120

25558850R00115

Printed in Great Britain
by Amazon